Sarah
from Grandma
Christmas 1990.

PRONUNCIATION KEY

Vowel sounds

a	as in **b**a**ckbone, **g**a**s, s**a**tellite
aa	as in f**a**thom, l**a**titude, pl**a**net
ah	as in f**au**na, f**o**ssil
ar	as in **ar**tery, b**ar**k, l**ar**va
aw	as in c**au**stic, l**aw**
ay	as in c**a**ve, d**ay**, v**ei**n
e	as in cr**e**st, d**e**sert, **e**nergy
ee	as in alg**ae**, b**e**havior, ch**e**mistry, degr**ee**, **ear**drum, n**u**trient
er	as in ast**er**oid, c**ir**cle, **ear**th, mixt**ure**, w**or**k
ew	as in comp**u**ter, d**ew**, n**eu**ron
i	as in amph**i**bian, an**i**mal, m**i**neral
o	as in b**o**tany, f**o**g, m**o**llusk
oh	as in b**o**ne, **o**zone, sn**ow**
oo	as in l**u**nar, sch**oo**l
or	as in c**or**ona, f**ore**cast, p**ore**
ow	as in cl**ou**d, c**o**mpound
oy	as in all**oy**, s**oi**l
u	as in **a**tom, bl**oo**d, n**e**rvous, r**u**st
uh	as in **au**rora, m**o**lecule, v**i**sible, st**e**thoscope
y	as in b**i**osphere, h**y**pothesis, l**i**ght

Consonant sounds

b	as in a**b**sorb, **b**ulb, ne**b**ula
ch	as in ha**tch**, na**t**ural, **n**iche
d	as in be**d**rock, col**d**, **d**ensity
f	as in coni**f**er, diaphra**gm**, **f**orest
g	as in e**gg**, fo**g**, **g**alaxy
h	as in **h**eredity, **h**orizon
j	as in carti**l**age, ener**gy**, **j**et, ri**dge**
k	as in **c**orona, e**c**lipse, **k**ingdom
l	as in **l**eaf, paral**l**el
m	as in **m**a**mm**al, o**m**nivore
n	as in a**n**imal, fu**n**gus, **n**ebula
ng	as in freezi**ng**
p	as in ca**p**illary, **p**lant, telesco**p**e
r	as in fo**r**est, **r**etina, t**r**ansistor
s	as in **c**ircuit, ga**s**, **s**tem
sh	as in fi**sh**, **g**lacier
ss	as in compa**ss**, fluore**sc**ence, respon**se**
t	as in bo**t**any, neu**t**ron, **t**ornado
th	as in fa**th**om, s**t**e**th**oscope, **th**eory
v	as in ca**v**e, con**v**ex, **v**enom
w	as in s**q**uare, **w**ater
z	as in len**s**, oo**z**e, **z**ero
zh	as in fi**ss**ion, illu**s**ion, mira**g**e

The Kids' Science Dictionary

NOTE TO THE READER

Are you ever amazed at how often science is in the news? Almost every day a new technological advance makes headlines. We hear about supernovae and solar energy, gamma rays and galaxies, magnets and Mach 1—but what *are* all these things? What do the sciences of physics, botany, and paleontology really involve? With technology affecting our lives more and more all the time, it is necessary for everyone to be aware of the world of science. *The Kids' Science Dictionary* contains more than 700 scientific terms that will help you discover new words, and better understand the world around you. Illustrations and examples are given and definitions are clear and simple.

Science is exciting and fun. *The Kids' Science Dictionary* will help you at school and at home with science projects and homework.

HOW TO USE THIS DICTIONARY

The Kids' Science Dictionary gives the *scientific* definitions of words and terms. Some words have more than one meaning, and you can check the regular dictionary for other definitions.

The letter in italics next to each defined word names the part of speech:

n. means noun, a name word
v. means verb, an action word
adj. means adjective, a descriptive word.

A phonetic guide to pronunciation is included with each entry. The Pronunciation Key on the first page will help you sound out the words.

The Kids' Science Dictionary

By Q. L. Pearce
Illustrated by Kaye Quinn

CHECKERBOARD PRESS
NEW YORK

For Joslyn Hitter

Acknowledgments
Special thanks to Helene Chirinian, Sarina Simon, and Lisa Melton for their hard work and encouragement. Also, my gratitude to William J. Pearce, Ph.D., Assistant Professor of Physiology, Loma Linda University School of Medicine; Paul Komarnicki, science educator, Wayne Township (New Jersey) Public School System; and Edith Shine, Research Assistant, Department of Microbiology, Georgia Institute of Technology, for their diligent review of the dictionary.

Library of Congress Cataloging-in-Publication Data
Pearce, Q. L. (Querida Lee)
    The kids' science dictionary / by Q.L. Pearce ; illustrated by Kaye Quinn.
       p. cm.
    Summary: Defines scientific names and terms in simple language and illustrations.
    ISBN 0-02-689074-7
    1. Science—Dictionaries, Juvenile. [1. Science—Dictionaries.]
I. Quinn, Kaye, ill. II. Title.
Q123.P33 1988
503—dc19   88-71150
                                                  CIP
                                                  AC

Copyright © 1989 RGA Publishing Group. All rights reserved.
Published by Checkerboard Press, a division of Macmillan, Inc. Printed in U.S.A.
CHECKERBOARD PRESS and colophon are trademarks of Macmillan, Inc.

Aa

absolute zero (ab•soh•LOOT ZEE•roh) *n.* the lowest possible temperature. At absolute zero all molecular motion stops. Absolute zero is 0° on the Kelvin scale, −273° on the Celsius scale, and −460° on the Fahrenheit scale.

absorb (ab•ZORB) *v.* to soak up or take in liquids, gases, or energy.

acceleration (ak•SELL•uh•RAY•shun) *n.* the rate at which speed or velocity increases.

acid (AS•id) *n.* a chemical compound containing hydrogen. The concentration of hydrogen ions determines the strength of the acid. Acid solutions are corrosive.

acid rain (AS•id RAYN) *n.* acid rainwater results when rainwater in clouds mixes with harmful substances released into the atmosphere, usually by factories and automobiles. Acid rain can damage forests and lakes.

action (AK•shun) *n.* a force in one direction that causes an effect of equal but opposite force (a reaction).

adaptation (a•dap•TAY•shun) *n.* the changes living things make to survive under new circumstances. For example, unlike other bears, polar bears have hair on the bottom of their paws. This is an adaptation that makes it easier for them to walk on ice.

1

air mass (AYR MASS) *n.* a large body of air with the same temperature and water content throughout.

air pressure (AYR PRESH•er) *n.* the force exerted by the air in the atmosphere. The weight of air. It is about 14 lbs. per square inch at sea level. It decreases at higher altitudes.

albedo (al•BEE•doh) *n.* the degree to which something reflects the light that falls on it. An object with an albedo of 1 is a perfect reflector. An albedo of 0 is a black surface that reflects no light.

alcohol (AL•kuh•hol) *n.* a family of clear, colorless, liquid organic compounds containing carbon, oxygen, and hydrogen. Alcohols may be made from many substances including wood, grains, fruits, and chemicals.

algae (AL•jee) *n.* a large diverse group of plants. Most grow in water but some can be found on desert rocks and arctic snow. They do not have true leaves, stems, or roots.

Single celled *Sargassum* *Kelp*
Types of algae

alloy (AL•oy) *n.* a metal made up of a combination of two or more different metals. Bronze is an alloy of copper and tin.

alluvium (uh•LOO•vee•um) *n.* material carried in suspension by a river and deposited on a delta or floodplain.

altitude (AL•tih•tood) *n.* the height of an object, usually measured from sea level.

alveolus (al•VEE•uh•lus) *n.* a tiny balloonlike sac in the lungs of mammals. These sacs fill with air and exchange oxygen for carbon dioxide in blood vessels.

Alveoli

ampere (AM•peer) *n.* a standard unit of measure of electric current.

amphibian (am•FIB•ee•an) *n.* a cold-blooded animal that in its larval or tadpole stage lives in water and breathes through gills, and in its adult stage lives on land and breathes air.

Tadpole

Spring salamander **Amphibians** *Frog*

angle (AYN•gul) *n.* the amount of space between two lines or planes that meet each other. This space is measured in degrees (°). A right angle is one of 90°.

Right angle

animal (AN•ih•mul) *n.* a living creature able to move by itself. Unlike green plants, an animal cannot produce its own food.

Mammal *Fish*

Mammal **Animals** *Reptile* *Bird*

annual (AN•yew•ul) *adj.* happening once a year.

3

antenna (an•TEN•uh) *n.* one of the sensory feelers occurring in pairs on the heads of insects. The plural is antennae.

n. a length of conducting metal used to receive or send electromagnetic signals.

artery (AR•ter•ee) *n.* a vessel that carries blood away from the heart. Arteries are lined with a special type of muscle that helps to move the blood.

arthropod (AR•thruh•pod) *n.* an animal that has a jointed outer shell called an exoskeleton instead of bones. Crabs and insects are arthropods.

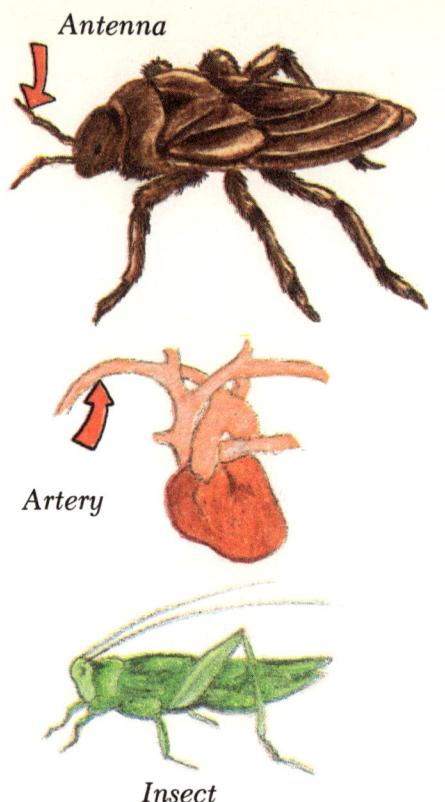

asteroid (AS•ter•oyd) *n.* a small mass of heavily cratered rock that orbits the sun. Most asteroids are less than one mile in diameter, but the asteroid Ceres is larger than six hundred miles in diameter.

asteroid belt (AS•ter•oyd BELT) *n.* an area in space between Mars and Jupiter where most asteroids are located.

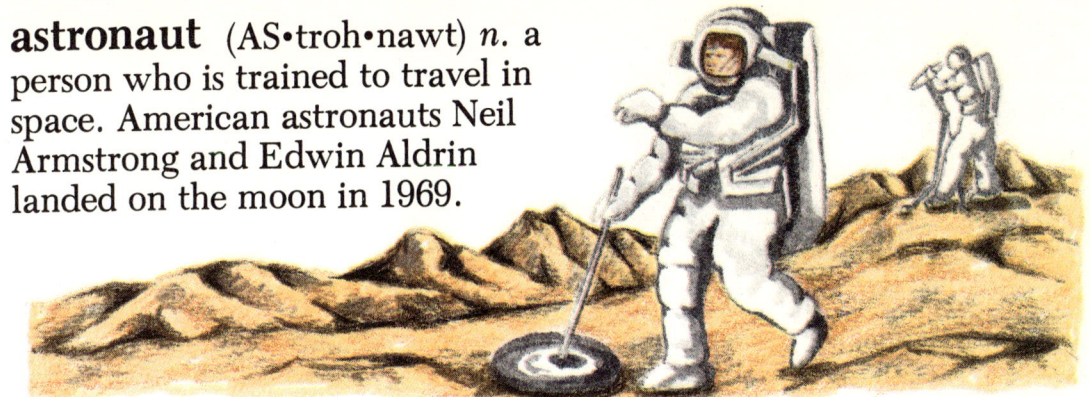

astronaut (AS•troh•nawt) *n.* a person who is trained to travel in space. American astronauts Neil Armstrong and Edwin Aldrin landed on the moon in 1969.

astronomical unit (as•troh•NOM•ih•kul YEW•nit) *n.* (AU) the average distance from the sun to the earth, about ninety-three million miles. AUs are often used to measure distance between objects within our solar system.

astronomy (as•TRON•oh•mee) *n.* the study of space beyond our atmosphere and all of the stars, satellites, and planets that it contains.

atmosphere (AT•muh•sfeer) *n.* a layer of gases around a planet or star. Earth's atmosphere is more than three hundred miles high.

atom (AT•um) *n.* the smallest unit of matter that cannot be divided by chemical reaction. Groups of atoms form molecules. An atom has a central nucleus with electrons spinning around it.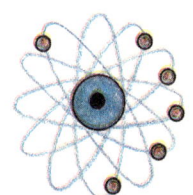

atrium (AY•tree•um) *n.* one of two chambers in the heart that receives blood from the veins.

aurora (uh•ROR•uh) *n.* glowing colored lights in the night sky at and near the polar regions, caused by charged particles from the solar wind interacting with the earth's magnetic field.

Rayed arc   *Flames*

Two types of auroras

5

axis (AKS•iss) *n.* an imaginary line on which a planet, star, or other object turns. The earth spins on its axis once every twenty-four hours.

Bb

backbone (BAK•bohn) *n.* a hollow chain of bones in the back of certain kinds of animals, which contains and protects the spinal cord and supports the body. Animals with backbones are called vertebrates.

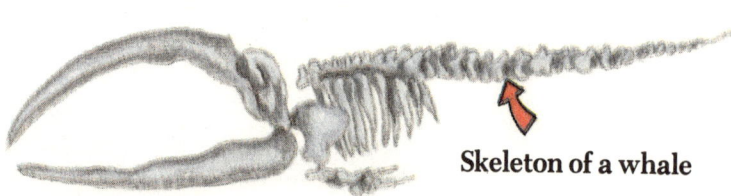
Skeleton of a whale

bacteria (bak•TEER•ee•uh) *n.* single-celled microscopic organisms. Some cause disease but many are helpful, aiding digestion and fermentation. A single organism is called a bacterium. The control of harmful bacteria has greatly increased life expectancy.

baleen (bay•LEEN) *n.* the long bony plates attached to the upper jaw of some whales. The animals use the plates to strain plankton and other food from seawater.

Baleen   Sei whale

bark (BARK) *n.* the tough outer covering on the trunk and branches of trees.

n. a short, sharp sound made by animals such as dogs and seals.

barometer (buh•RAH•muh•ter) *n.* an instrument used to measure atmospheric pressure.

base (BAYSS) *n. chemistry:* a substance that reacts with acid to form salt.

n. math: a line or surface on which a figure stands.

battery (BAT•er•ee) *n.* a collection of cells that convert energy, usually by chemical reaction, into electricity.

bedrock (BED•rok) *n.* a solid rock layer covered by layers of broken rock and soil.

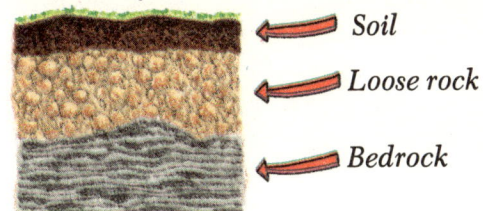

behavior (bee•HAYV•yor) *n.* the way living things act in relation to the environment. Animals are born with some behaviors, and others are learned.

biceps (BY•seps) *n.* large skeletal muscle found in the upper arm.

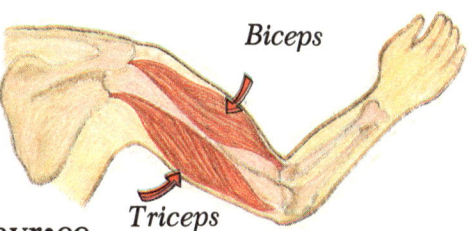

binary star (BY•nayr•ee STAR) *n.* two companion stars that are attracted to each other by gravity and rotate around a common point.

Binary star system

biology (by•OL•oh•jee) *n.* the study of living things.

biosphere (BY•oh•sfeer) *n.* the zone above and below the surface of the earth in which living organisms are known to exist.

bird (BERD) *n.* an animal that has a backbone and feathers and that lays eggs. Birds have wings, and most, but not all, can fly.

Ruby-throated hummingbird   *White stork*

bit (BIT) *n.* the smallest unit of memory storage in a computer.

bivalve (BY•valv) *n.* an animal with a two-part shell that opens and closes. Clams are bivalves.

Oyster
Clam

black hole (BLAK HOHL) *n.* a very small, extremely dense object in space with a gravitational pull so strong that not even light can escape from it.

blood vessel (BLUD VESS•ul) *n.* any flexible tube, such as a vein, artery, or capillary, that carries blood throughout the body.

Bohr, Niels (BOR, NEELZ) *1885–1962* Danish physicist who won the Nobel Prize in 1922. He discovered the quantum theory of the atom: that electrons orbiting an atom do so at specific levels. Bohr's later work helped to develop the atom bomb, and he worked hard to encourage the peaceful use of atomic power.

boiling point (BOYL•ing POYNT) *n.* the temperature at which a liquid becomes a gas.

bone cell (BOHN SELL) *n.* a living cell in the inner bone that produces the bone's hard outer covering.

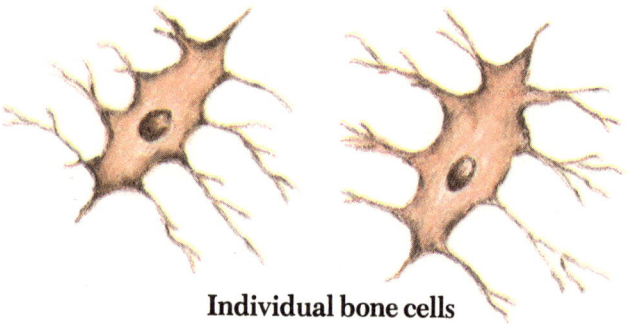
Individual bone cells

booster engine (BOO•ster EN•jin) *n.* The main engine of a rocket, used for launching it. May detach after use.

botany (BOT•uh•nee) *n.* the study of plants.

Boyle, Robert (BOYL, RAH•bert) *1627–1691* English chemist who proved that fire can't burn and sound can't be heard in a vacuum, and that air exerts pressure. He also defined chemical elements and compounds and proved that water expands when it freezes. He was one of the first scientists to prove his theories by experimentation.

bulb (BULB) *n.* the part of certain plants that lives underground and stores food. Tulips grow from bulbs.

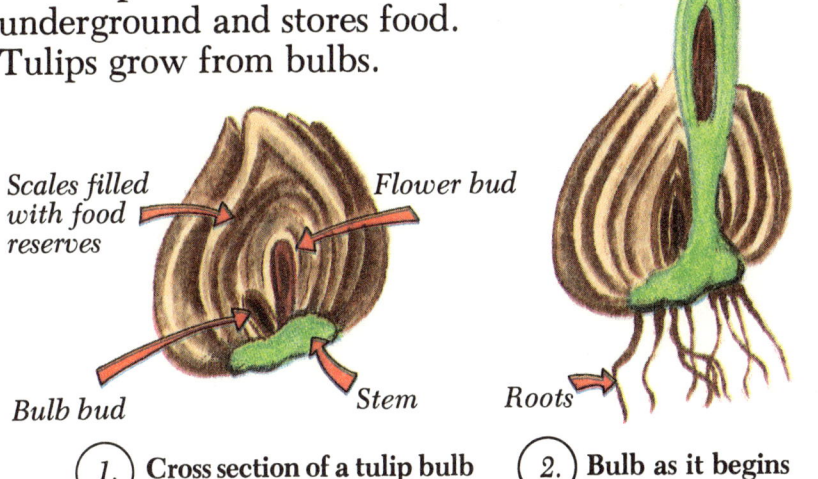

1. Cross section of a tulip bulb
2. Bulb as it begins to grow
3. Full-grown bulb 

n. a glass object with a wire inside that gives off light when electric current passes through it.

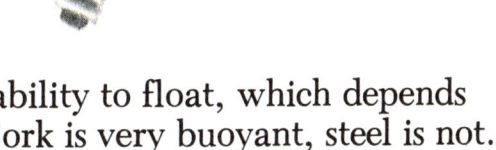

Electric light bulb

buoyancy (BOY•an•see) *n.* the ability to float, which depends on the ratio of weight to volume. Cork is very buoyant, steel is not. A ship made of steel, however, can float because of the air inside.

by-product (BY-PRAH•dukt) *n.* a secondary substance produced during a chemical reaction. The by-products of burning wood are gases and ashes; heat is the end product.

byte (BYT) *n.* a unit of computer memory made up of a certain number of bits.

Cc

calorie (KAL•or•ee) *n.* a unit of heat measurement. The amount of heat energy it takes to raise one gram of water 1° centigrade or Celsius.

cambium (KAM•bee•um) *n.* a thin layer of growing cells in the stem of many plants. As new cells are produced by the cambium, the stem grows thicker.

camouflage (KAM•oh•flazh) *n.* patterns and coloring some animals have developed enabling them to hide by blending in with their surroundings.

Banded iguana

canyon (KAN•yun) *n.* a deep cut in rock, usually carved out by a flowing river.

capillary (KAP•ih•layr•ee) *n.* One of many tiny vessels, having the diameter the size of a red blood cell, which carry blood to all parts of the body. Capillaries connect veins to arteries.

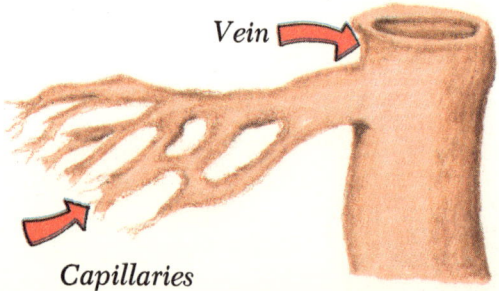
Vein
Capillaries

carbohydrate (kar•boh•HY•drayt) *n.* sugars and starches made by plants and used by animals as food. Carbohydrates are made up of carbon, hydrogen, and oxygen.

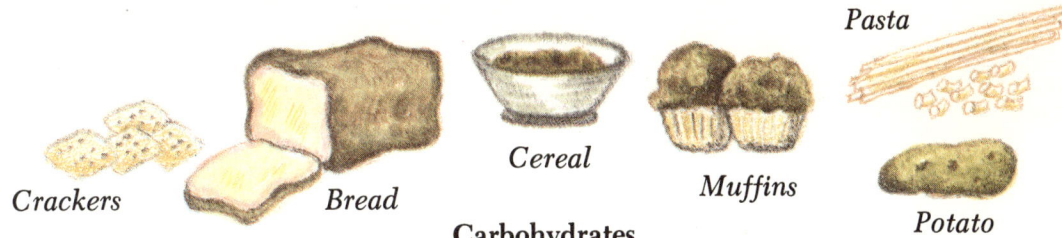

Crackers *Bread* *Cereal* *Muffins* *Pasta* *Potato*

Carbohydrates

carbon (KAR•bon) *n.* element that is a building block of life. It combines easily with many other elements and takes many forms. Diamonds and coal are made of carbon. Your body also contains large amounts of carbon.

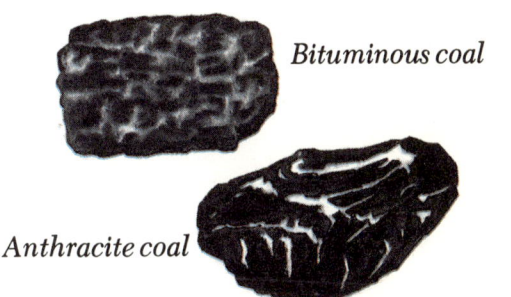

Bituminous coal

Anthracite coal

carbon dioxide (KAR•bon dy•OKS•eyed) *n.* a gas made of carbon and oxygen atoms. Plants use carbon dioxide from the air to make food from sunlight (photosynthesis). Animals release carbon dioxide when they exhale.

carnivore (KAR•nih•vor) *n.* flesh-eating animal such as a lion or wolf.

Lion *Hyena* *Nile crocodile*

Carnivores

11

cartilage (KAR•tih•lij) *n.* in animals, connective tissue that functions like a bone but is elastic. This flexible material forms the human nose and ears.

catalyst (KAT•uh•list) *n.* a substance that causes or speeds up a chemical reaction but is not changed by that reaction.

caterpillar (KAT•er•pil•er) *n.* a butterfly or moth goes through four stages from egg to adult. The second stage, or larva, is a caterpillar.

Caterpillar

caudal (KAWD•ul) *adj.* of or near the tail. A shark's tail has two caudal fins.

Caudal fins

Caudal fins

Sand tiger shark

White shark

caustic (KAWS•tik) *adj.* having the ability to burn, corrode, or destroy.

cave (KAYV) *n.* a natural hollow space in the earth, often on the side of a hill or mountain, with an opening to the surface.

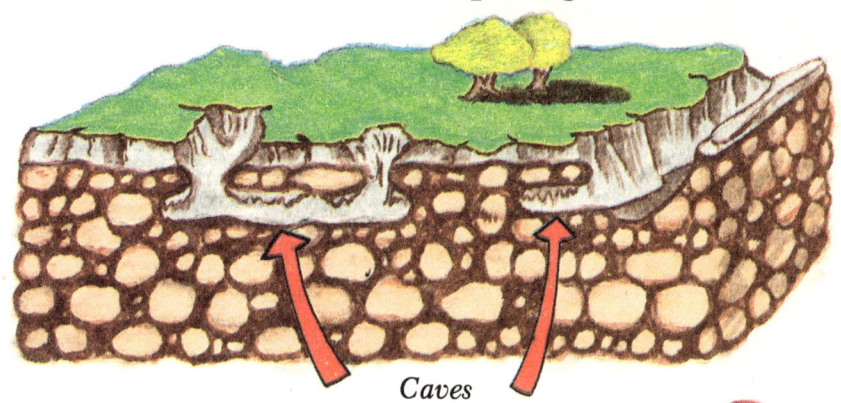
Caves

cell (SELL) *n.* the smallest living unit that makes up the whole or part of living tissue in plants and animals.

cell division (SELL dih•VIH•zhun) *n.* the method by which many cells reproduce. One cell divides in half to make two identical cells, which in turn divide. When the cell divides, each new cell has all the genetic material the original cell had.

cell membrane (SELL MEM•brayn) *n.* a thin, fatty protective barrier around a cell. It lets needed material pass into the cell and allows wastes to pass out.

cell wall (SELL WAHL) *n.* a tough protective layer composed usually of cellulose around the outer membrane of bacteria, fungi, and green plants.

cellulose (SELL•yew•lohss) *n.* the material that makes up cell walls in plants.

Celsius (SEL•see•us) *adj.* a temperature scale in which 0° Celsius is the freezing point of water and 100° Celsius is the boiling point of water. The Celsius scale is named after Anders Celsius, a scientist who lived in the 1700s. Today, the Celsius scale is also known as the centigrade scale.

centigrade (SEN•tih•grayd) *adj.* a scale for measuring temperature based on the boiling and freezing points of water. It freezes at 0° and boils at 100°. Centigrade is also called Celsius.

centimeter (SEN•tih•mee•ter) *n.* a unit of measure of length in the metric system. It equals one-hundreth ($\frac{1}{100}$) of a meter. One inch equals 2.58 centimeters.

centrifugal force (sen•TRIH•foo•gul FORSS) *n.* the force that acts on an object moving in a circular path, pushing it outward.

cerebellum (ser•uh•BELL•um) *n.* the part of the brain that controls balance and coordination.

cerebrum (suh•REE•brum) *n.* the large part of the brain which controls the senses, speech, and thought.

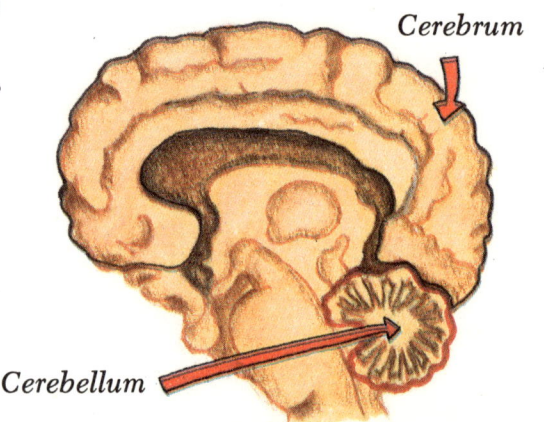

chain reaction (CHAYN ree•AK•shun) *n.* a series of events in which each event is the result of the previous event and the cause of the next event. A line of dominoes falling is a chain reaction, and so is nuclear fission when there is enough fuel.

chemical energy (KEM•ih•kul EN•er•jee) *n.* energy a substance possesses by virtue of its composition. In a fire, chemical energy is released as heat and light.

chemistry (KEM•uh•stree) *n.* the study of the composition and properties of substances that make up our world.

chitin (KYT•in) *n.* the tough, semitransparent substance that forms the principle part of crustacean and insect shells.

chlorophyll (KLOR·oh·fill) *n.* a green substance in plants that reacts with sunlight and is used to manufacture food by photosynthesis.

chloroplast (KLOR·oh·plast) *n.* the part of plant cells that contains chlorophyll and other substances necessary for photosynthesis to take place.

Cross section of leaf cells

chromosomes (KROH·moh·somz) *n.* tiny, paired, threadlike objects in the nucleus of a cell. The chromosomes contain DNA, a substance that makes up genes. Genes determine the characteristics of each cell. They are inherited from parents.

chromosphere (KROH·moh·sfeer) *n.* the inner atmosphere of the sun.

cilia (SIL·ee·uh) *n.* tiny hairlike structures that grow out of some cells. Cilia beat in a wavelike motion. One-celled creatures use them to move. In some animals, cilia help move things inside the body. The human throat is lined with cilia that move dust particles away from the lungs.

Cells lining throat

circle (SER·kul) *n.* a collection of points which are all the same distance from a common central point. A circle is a flat two-dimensional figure.

circuit (SER·kit) *n.* the circular path of electric current through conductors, from the source of energy and back.

circulatory system (SER·kew·luh·tor·ee SIS·tem) *n.* the system of organs and tissues, including the heart and blood vessels, which moves blood through the body.

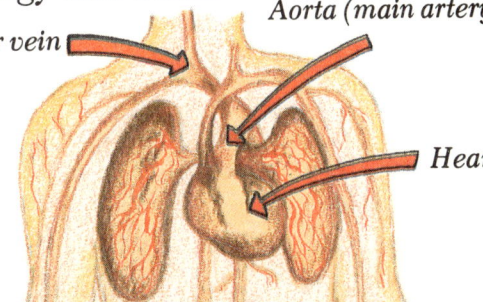

Section of circulatory system

circumference (ser•KUM•frenss)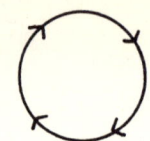
n. the distance around a circle.

cirrus (SER•us) *adj.* wispy clouds high in the sky made up of tiny ice crystals.

class (KLASS) *n.* a group of things that are alike in some important ways. Mammals, for instance, form one class of animals.

climate (KLY•mut) *n.* the average weather in an area over a long period of time. The climate in southern California, for example, is usually sunny and warm.

clouds (KLOWDZ) *n.* masses of water droplets and ice crystals in the atmosphere. Clouds are classified by their shape and distance from the ground.

Types of clouds

coal (KOHL) *n.* a solid, black mineral used as fuel. Coal consists mostly of carbon that formed over millions of years from decayed plants.

cohesion (koh•HEE•zhun) *n.* the force between particles that holds a substance or body together.

cold-blooded (KOLD BLUD•ed) *adj.* used to describe an animal that cannot control its body temperature. The temperature of the body changes with the temperature of the outside environment. Fish and reptiles are cold-blooded.

cold front (KOLD FRUNT) *n.* the place in the atmosphere along which a mass of cold air meets a mass of warm air, causing the warm air to rise.

combine (kom•BYN) *v.* to blend together. Atoms of hydrogen and oxygen combine to form water.

comet (KOM•et) *n.* a body of ice, gas, and dust in orbit around the sun. When it comes close enough to the sun, a comet develops a huge, glowing halo and long tail.

compass (KOM•pass) *n.* an instrument with a magnetic needle that always points toward the North Pole. A compass is used to show direction.

compound (KOM•pownd) *n.* atoms of two or more elements that have joined together to form a new substance. Common salt is a compound formed when sodium and chloride combine.

compress (kom•PRESS) *v.* to squeeze together.

computer (kom•PEWT•er) *n.* an electronic device that can accept information and then store, retrieve, and analyze it.

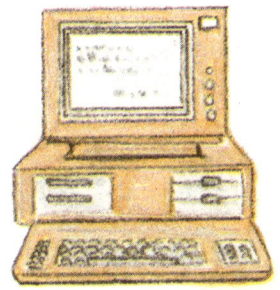

concave (kon•CAYV) *adj.* curved inward.

17

concentration (kon•sen•TRAY•shun) *n.* the amount per unit volume of a substance dissolved in a liquid or suspended in air.

condensation (kon•den•SAY•shun) *n.* drops of liquid that form when a gas changes into a liquid. Dew is made of water vapor condensed onto grass or other cool surfaces.

condense (kon•DENSS) *v.* to make something more dense or compact, such as to make a gas into a liquid.

v. to become liquid or solid.

conductor (kon•DUK•ter) *n.* a material through which energy moves quickly.

cone (COHN) *n.* one of the tiny color-sensitive cells in the inner lining of the eye.

n. multiple fruit of the pine or fir tree.

n. a geometric shape.

The human eye

conglomerate (kon•GLOM•er•ut) *n.* a sedimentary rock containing large rounded fragments of other rocks.

White pine tree branch

Conglomerate rock

18

conifer (KON•ih•fer) *n.* any of the numerous, chiefly evergreen trees or shrubs including the pine, fir, spruce, and other cone-producing plants.

coniferous (koh•NIF•er•us) *adj.* a tree that produces cones. Pines are coniferous trees.

conserve (kon•SERV) *v.* to use something carefully so as not to waste it. Survival of the human race, for example, depends on protecting and conserving the natural resources of the earth.

constellation (kon•stuh•LAY•shun) *n.* a group of stars that make up a recognizable pattern and have been given a name.

continental shelf (kon•tih•NEN•tal SHELF) *n.* the portion of the land beneath the ocean that slopes away from the shore and out to sea.

contract (kon•TRAKT) *v.* to become smaller.

convection (kon•VEK•shun) *n.* the transfer of heat in a liquid or gas by the circular movement of the heated portion of the liquid or gas. The movement is called the convection current. In a large container of water heated at the bottom, the hot water rises from the bottom to the top, where it is cooled and sinks again.

Convex

convex (kon•VEKS) *adj.* curved outward.

Copernicus, Nicolaus (koh•PER•nih•kus, NIK•laws) 1473–1543 Polish mathematician and astronomer. Because of his observation of the stars and planets, Copernicus concluded that the sun is the center of the universe—not the earth, as was then believed. Copernicus theorized that the earth revolves on its axis and is in orbit around the sun.

19

core (KOR) *n.* the inside of an object. The core of the sun is composed of super-hot hydrogen and helium gases.

corona (kor•OH•nuh) *n.* the outer atmosphere of the sun.

countdown (KOWNT•down) *n.* the period of time before the launch of a space vehicle when a final systems check is carried out. The time is usually counted backward, with zero being the launch time.

crater (KRAY•ter) *n.* a bowl-shaped hole in the ground. Craters can be caused by meteorites or volcanic eruptions.

crest (KREST) *n.* the highest point. The crest of a wave is the foaming top; the crest of a mountain is the highest ridge line going up to the peak.

crop (KROP) *n.* the product obtained from some cultivated plants. The word describes the growing or harvested plant that is later used for consumption.

n. a pouch in a bird's neck used to store food.

crust (KRUST) *n.* the outer layer of the earth. If the earth were the size of an egg, the crust would be about as thick as the eggshell.

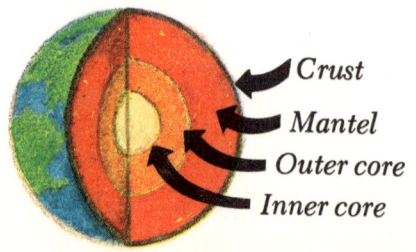

View of the center of the earth

20

crustacean (krus•TAY•shun) *n.* the class of animals with a hard, jointed outer shell, such as a crab or lobster.

Lobster   *Rock crab*

crystal (KRIS•tal) *n.* the form of certain solid substances. Crystals usually have flat faces and straight edges, which always meet at the same angles.

Hexagonal crystals

cube (KEWB) *n.* a six-sided figure, each face of which is the same size and all interior angles are 90°.

Cube

cumulus (KEW•mew•lus) *adj.* light, fluffy, rounded clouds.

Curie, Marie (KEW•ree, mah•REE) *1867–1934* French physicist. In 1903 she shared a Nobel prize for physics with her husband, Pierre Curie, and Henri Becquerel for the discovery of the chemical element radium. In 1911 she won a Nobel prize for chemistry for further work with radium. Her research is the basis of radiology, the study of radioactive materials.

21

current (KUR•ent) *n.* the flow of gas or liquid. The Gulf Stream is a warm current of water in the Atlantic Ocean.

n. the flow of electrons through a circuit. A common unit of measure of current is the ampere.

cytoplasm (SYT•oh•plaz•um) *n.* a complex mixture of water, salt, and organic materials that fills living cells; often in a jellylike state.

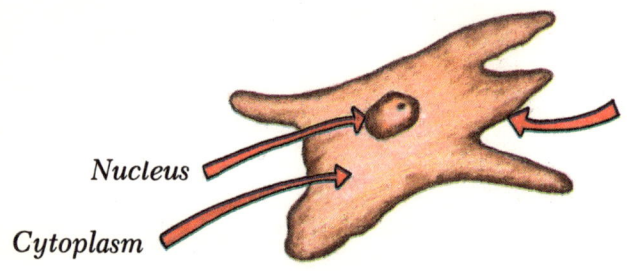

Human connective tissue cell

Dalton, John (DAWL•tun, JON) *1766–1844* English physicist who theorized that all matter is made up of tiny particles called atoms. He stated that these atoms can combine in many ways to create different chemical compounds, but the atoms themselves remain unchanged. He made the first table of atomic weights.

Darwin, Charles (DAR•win, CHARLZ) *1809–1882* English naturalist. In his book, *On the Origin of the Species*, he said that only the healthiest animals tend to survive and pass on their traits to their young. He called this natural selection. Also, as the environment changes, only those living things that can adapt to the changes will survive. He called this process adaptation.

decay (dee•KAY) *v.* to break down into a simpler form or substance. To break down, deteriorate, or rot.

deciduous (dih•SID•yew•us) *adj.* shedding annually. Many deciduous trees and shrubs lose their leaves in fall.

degree (duh•GREE) *n.* a unit of measurement, as of temperature or pressure, marked off on the scale of a measuring instrument. The symbol for degree is (°).

n. a unit of measurement of angles and circles. A circle is made up of 360°.

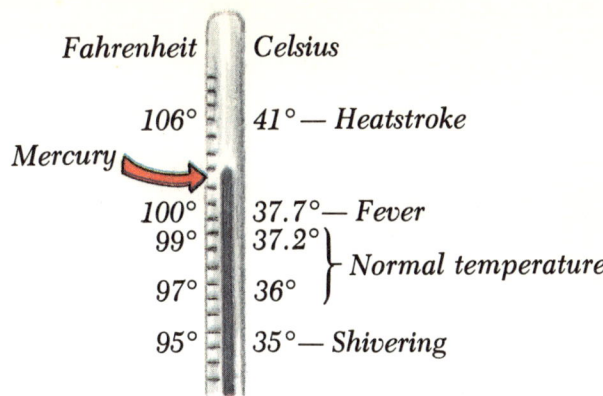
Thermometer measuring body temperature

delta (DEL•tuh) *n.* the area at the mouth of a river made up of sand and silt deposited by the river.

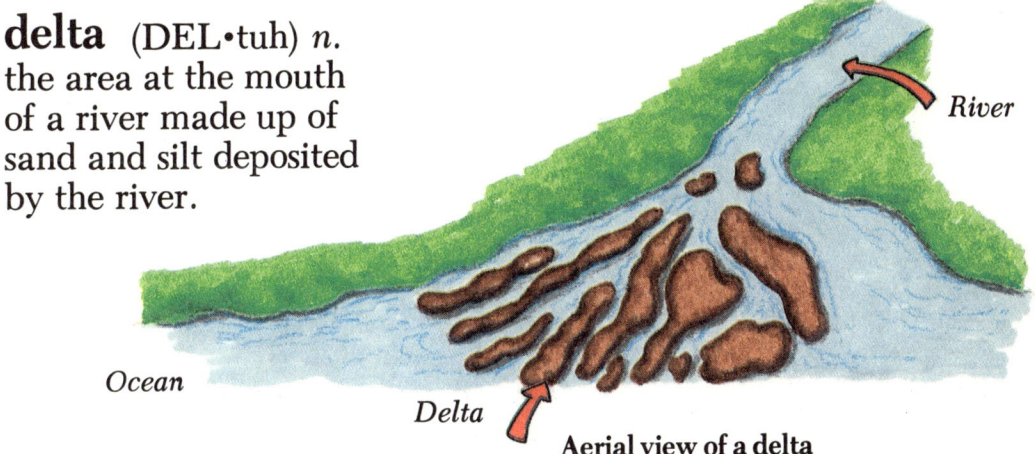
Aerial view of a delta

den (DEN) *n.* the shelter or home of certain wild animals such as bears and wolves.

density (DEN•sit•ee) *n.* the ratio of weight to volume. If two objects are the same size but one is more dense, the dense object is heavier.

deposit (dih•POZ•it) *n.* matter that is left behind after being moved by forces such as wind and water.

v. to leave something behind.

Descartes, Rene (day•KART, ruh•NAY) *1596–1650* French philosopher who discovered the law of light refraction—light bends when it moves from one substance to another. He also developed the Cartesian method of study: Break a problem into parts, solve the easiest part first and the hardest part last, then outline all the results and study them carefully.

23

desert (DEZ·ert) *n.* a barren area, often covered with sand or rock, that has a dry climate.

dew (DEW) *n.* drops of water that form on cold surfaces as the air around them cools. Dew usually forms on grass during the night.

diameter (dy·AM·ih·ter) *n.* the distance of a straight line through the center of a circle or sphere from one side to the other.

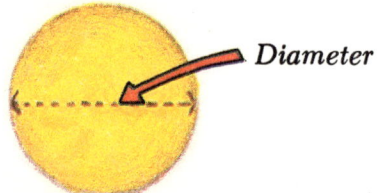

diaphragm (DY·uh·fram) *n.* a wall of muscle below the lungs that moves and causes air pressure in the chest to change, making it possible to breathe. The diaphragm separates the chest cavity from the abdominal cavity.

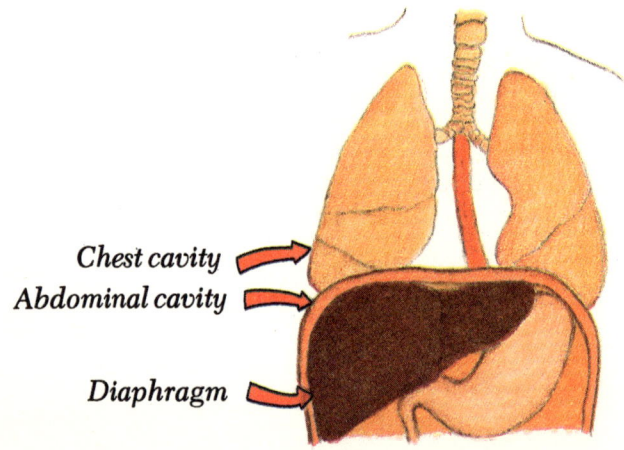

diet (DY·et) *n.* the kind of food an animal usually eats.

diffusion (dih•FEW•zhun) *n.* the method by which certain substances cross cell membranes to enter or leave the cell.

n. the movement of molecules of a material throughout the molecules of another, such as perfume diffusing through the air.

n. the scattering of light rays which are reflected by an irregular surface.

digestion (dy•JES•chun) *n.* the process of breaking down food into a form that the cells can absorb and use.

digestive system (dy•JES•tiv SIS•tem) *n.* the parts of the body used in the digestive process. The system includes the alimentary canal, the liver, and the pancreas.

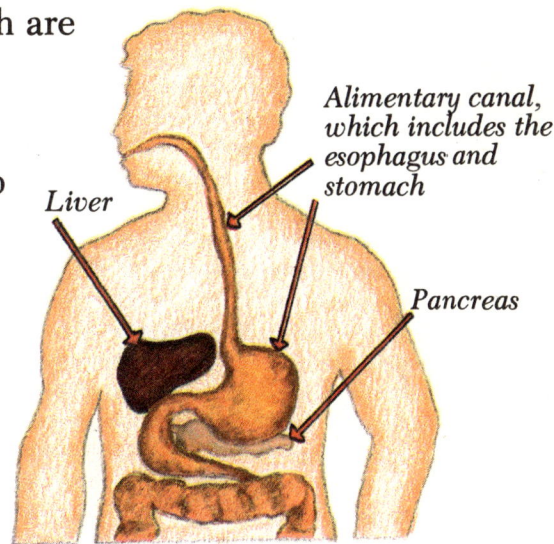

The digestive system

direct ray (dy•REKT RAY) *n.* a ray of light that comes directly from its source and strikes a surface. We see direct rays of the sun during the day, and rays of sunlight reflected off the moon at night.

dissolve (diz•AHLV) *v.* to break up and disperse evenly throughout a liquid. Sugar will dissolve in water.

distillation (dis•till•AY•shun) *n.* the process of purifying a liquid through evaporation and condensation. Distillation is also used to separate mixtures of liquids with different boiling points.

diurnal (dy•ER•nul) *adj.* used to describe events or activities that take place during the day; daily.

DNA *n.* the abbreviation of **deoxyribonucleic acid** (dee•OK•see•ry•boh•noo•KLAY•ik AS•id), the material within living cells that carries genetic information in almost all life forms.

doldrums (DOHL•drumz) *n.* an area of calm weather near the equator.

25

Doppler effect (DOPP·ler ih·FEKT) *n.* the apparent change in frequency of an energy wave due to motion between the source of the wave and the observer. The way that the sound of a train whistle seems to change as it approaches and then passes an observer is an example of this.

dormant (DOR·mant) *adj.* used to describe a living thing that is in a resting stage. Many plants remain dormant through the winter.

Full bloom in spring Dormant in winter

dorsal (DOR·sul) *adj.* of or near the back; along the backbone. Many types of fish have dorsal fins.

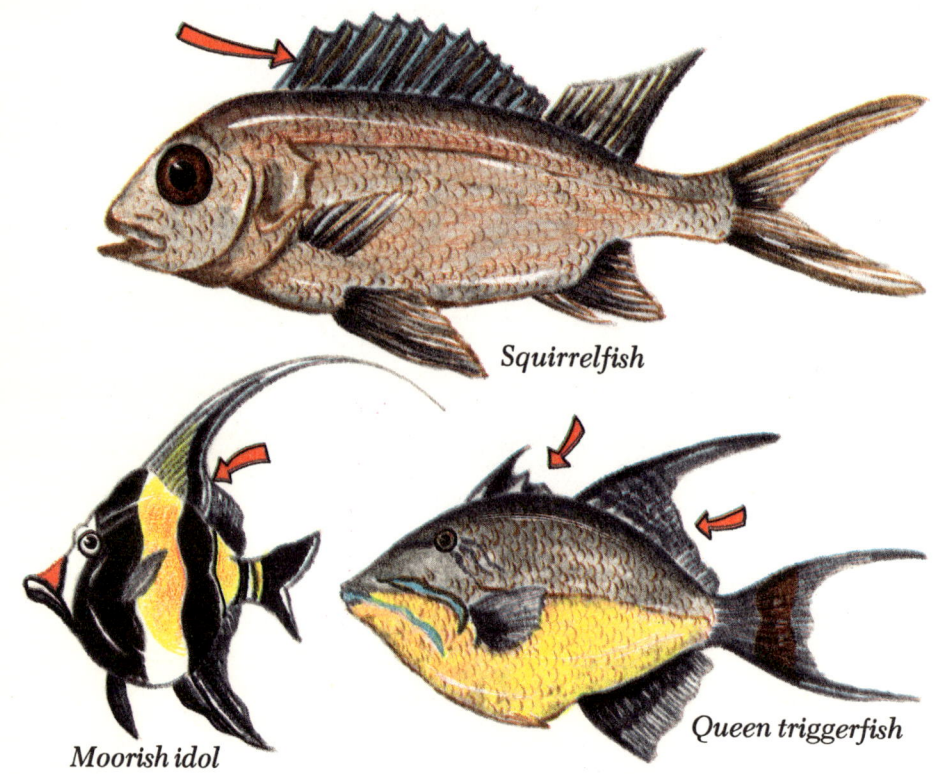

Squirrelfish

Moorish idol *Queen triggerfish*

The dorsal fins of various fish

drug (DRUG) *n.* a chemical substance used to cause a change in a living organism.

dry cell (DRY SELL) *n.* a battery made up of a zinc case with a carbon rod inside. Most toys operate on dry cell batteries.

duct (DUKT) *n.* a tube that carries a gas or a liquid. There are ducts in buildings and also in most plants and animals.

Cross section of a stem

dune (DOON) *n.* a sand hill or ridge formed by the wind, usually in desert regions or near lakes and oceans.

Ee

eardrum (EER•drum) *n.* the thin membrane between the outer ear and the inner ear. It vibrates when sound waves strike it.

Parts of the human ear

Earth (ERTH) *n.* third planet from the sun. The only planet in the solar system known to support life, and the planet on which we live.

n. solid matter composed of rock and sand; ground.

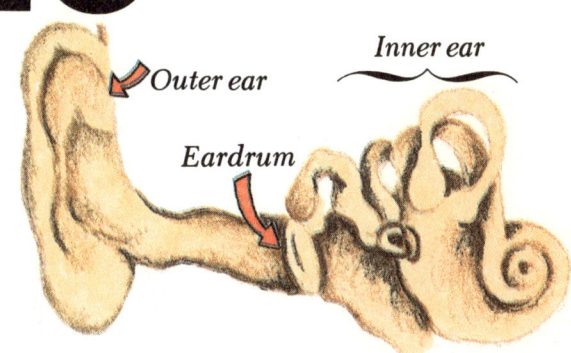
The planets of our solar system

earthquake (ERTH•kwayk) *n.* a sudden movement of a portion of the earth's crust.

echo (EK•oh) *n.* the return or repetition of a sound that has bounced off a surface such as a hill, a cave, or a wall and back to its source.

27

eclipse (ee•KLIPS) *n.* the obscuring of light from one object to another by something located between them. A lunar eclipse occurs when the earth comes between the sun and the moon. A solar eclipse occurs when the moon comes between the earth and the sun.

v. to block the light from a source.

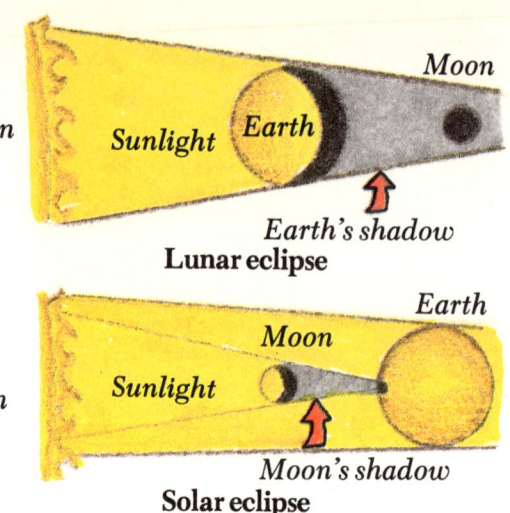
Lunar eclipse

Solar eclipse

ecology (ee•KOL•oh•jee) *n.* the study of how living things relate to each other and to their environment.

egg (EGG) *n.* a female reproductive cell.

Einstein, Albert (EYN•styn, AL•bert) *1879–1955* American physicist known for his theory of relativity. This states that time, motion, and distance must be measured in terms of one another. For example, the time you exist in depends on how fast you are moving. He also theorized that the speed of light is the same in all parts of the universe, and that mass can be expressed in terms of energy and energy in terms of mass.

electricity (ih•lek•TRISS•ih•tee) *n.* energy generated by the flow of electric current.

electromagnet (ih•lek•troh•MAG•net) *n.* a conductor that behaves like a magnet when electricity flows through a coil of wire surrounding the conductor.

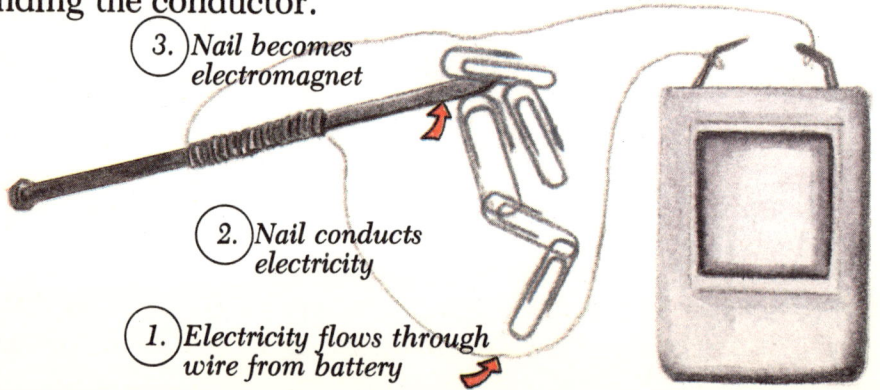
A nail becomes an electromagnet

electromagnetic energy (ih•LEK•troh•mag•NET•ik EN•er•jee) *n.* radiation that travels in waves, which have both electrical and magnetic properties. The electromagnetic spectrum is made up of many different forms of radiation, including X-rays, ultraviolet radiation, visible light, infrared radiation, and radio waves.

electron (ih•LEK•tron) *n.* a negatively charged particle of matter. Electrons may orbit the nucleus of an atom, or move freely through space.

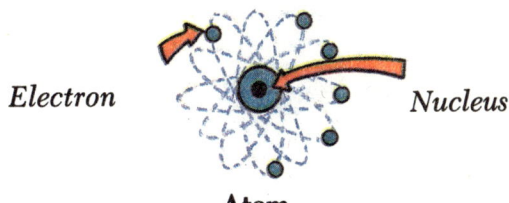

element (EL•uh•ment) *n.* a substance made up of only one kind of atom. Pure carbon and gold are elements.

ellipse (ih•LIPS) *n.* a flattened oval shape that has two fixed points (foci) instead of one central point, as in a circle. The planets move around the sun in elliptical orbits, the sun being at one focus.

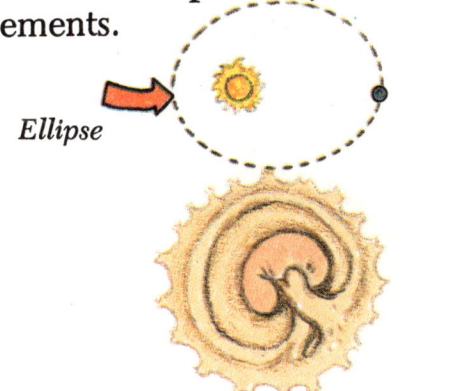

Human embryo—first month

embryo (em•BREE•oh) *n.* one of the earliest stages in the development of a fertilized egg.

endangered species (en•DAYN•jerd SPEE•seez) *n.* a group of living things that may die out if protective measures are not taken.

Blue whale
Galapagos turtle
Orangutan
Panda
Endangered species

energy (EN•er•jee) *n.* the capacity to do work, such as move an object. Energy can be changed to a different form but it cannot be destroyed.

29

environment (en•VY•ron•ment) *n.* the surroundings and conditions in which plants and animals live.

enzymes (EN•zymz) *n.* proteins in the body that are catalysts for many chemical reactions. Enzymes are helpful in the digestion of food.

epicenter (EP•ih•sent•er) *n.* the point on Earth's surface that is above the focus of an earthquake. Usually the most damage occurs at the epicenter of an earthquake.

epoch (EP•uk) *n.* a unit of geological time that is marked by distinct features and events.

equation (ih•KWAY•zhun) *n.* a mathematical description of an equal relationship between or among two or more things.

equator (ih•KWAY•ter) *n.* an imaginary line around the earth, halfway between the poles. This area receives direct rays from the sun and is very warm.

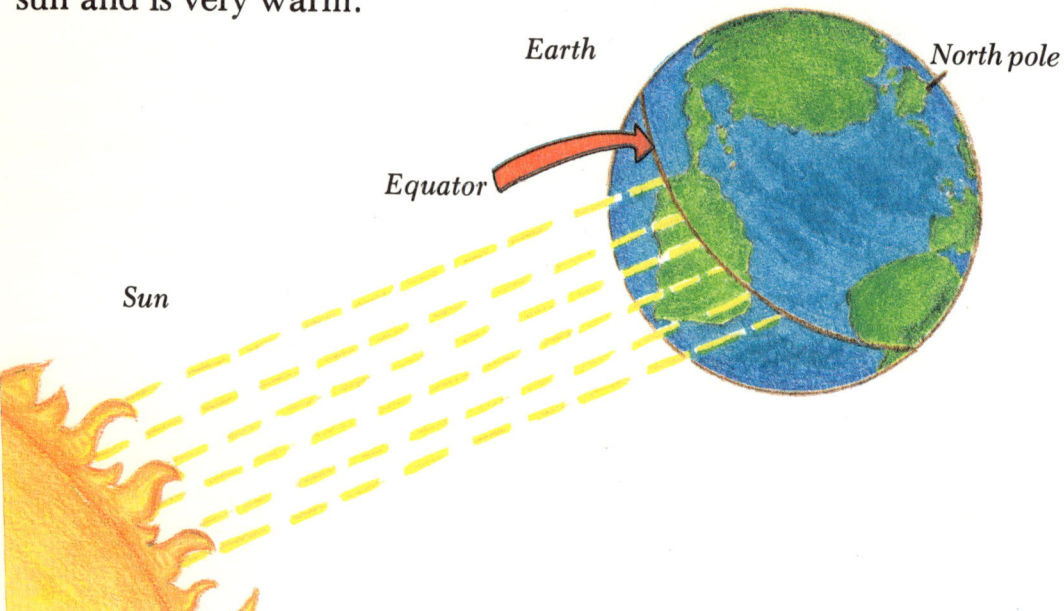

The warming of the equator

equilibrium (ee•kwih•LIB•ree•um) *n.* a point at which forces or effects are in balance.

equinox (EE•kwih•noks) *n.* one of the two points during the year when day and night are equal in length. It occurs in Spring around March 21 and in Fall around September 21.

era (EER•uh) *n.* the largest unit of measure of geological time.

erosion (ih•ROH•zhun) *n.* the wearing away of rocks and soil by natural forces such as wind and rain.

Erosion by wind

Waves eroding the coastline

escape velocity (es•KAYP vuh•LAHS•ih•tee) *n.* the speed a body must reach to break away from the pull of the earth's gravity.

estuary (ES•chew•ayr•ee) *n.* the mouth of a river where it meets the sea. Salt and fresh water mix in an estuary.

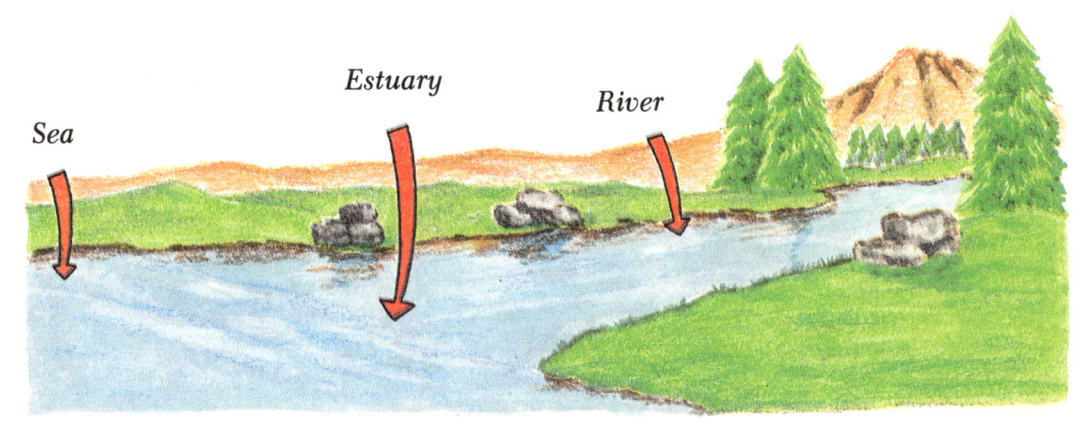

Sea *Estuary* *River*

evaporate (ih•VAP•uh•rayt) *v.* to change from a liquid to a gas without necessarily reaching the boiling point, through heating or the motion of air.

evolution (ev•oh•LOO•shun) *n.* a process of gradual change in the genetic makeup of a species, resulting from the reproductive success of the individuals best suited to survive the conditions at hand.

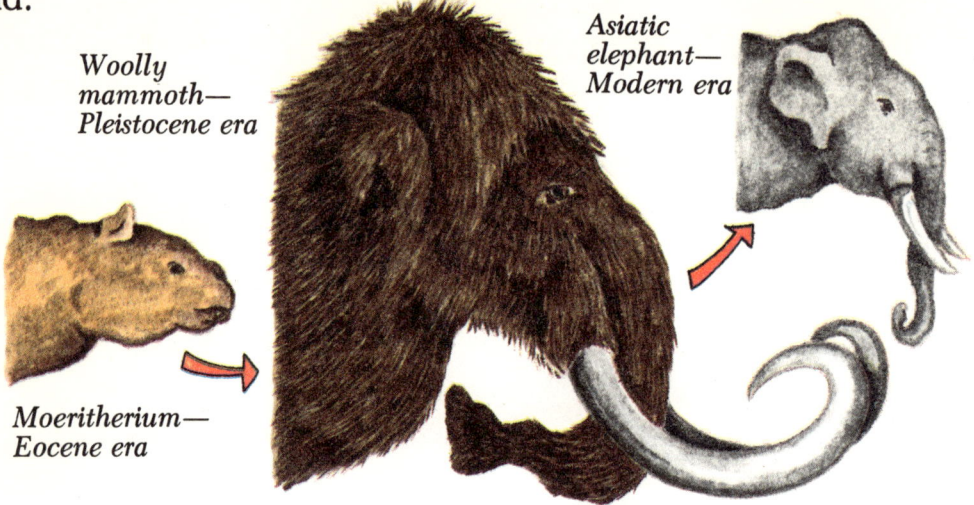

Asiatic elephant— Modern era

Woolly mammoth— Pleistocene era

Moeritherium— Eocene era

Evolution of the elephant

excretory system (EK•scruh•tor•ee SIS•tem) *n.* the system of the body that disposes of waste products.

exosphere (EK•soh•sfeer) *n.* the outer atmosphere of the earth.

expand (ek•SPAND) *v.* to swell or become larger.

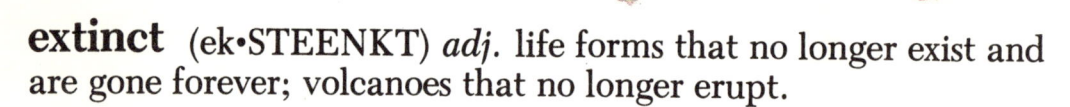

extinct (ek•STEENKT) *adj.* life forms that no longer exist and are gone forever; volcanoes that no longer erupt.

Notharctus lived in Wyoming fifty million years ago.

The Great Auk lived in the North Atlantic Ocean. The last pair was killed near Iceland in June 1844.

Extinct animals

Ff

Fahrenheit (FAYR•en•hyt) *adj.* a temperature scale at which water freezes at 32° and boils at 212°.

Faraday, Michael (FAYR•uh•day, MY•kul) *1791–1867* English physicist. He discovered the laws of electromagnetism (a magnetic field is created around a substance when electricity passes through it). He was able to liquify certain gases and discovered benzene, a chemical used as a solvent and a fuel. He invented the words *cathode*, *ion*, and *electrode*.

fathom (FAA•thum) *n.* a measure of depth in water. One fathom equals six feet. Originally it was the span of a man's arms.

fats (FATS) *n.* natural, solid compounds that are developed in plants and animals and are used as food or to store energy until needed. A liquid fat is called an oil.

fault (FAHLT) *n.* a break or crack in rock in the earth's crust; where two plates meet. When two plates move rapidly alongside each other they cause earthquakes.

fauna (FAH•nuh) *n.* the types of animals that live in a particular area.

Arctic fox
Harp seal
Walrus
Polar bear
Animals of the Arctic

Fermi, Enrico (FAYR•mee, en•REE•koh) *1901–1954*
American Italian-born physicist who won a Nobel prize in 1938. His work paved the way for controlled nuclear fission—splitting the nuclei of atoms into parts, which releases energy. In 1942 he directed the operation of the first nuclear reactor.

fertilizer (FER•til•eye•zer) *n.* nutrients added to soil to help plants grow.

filament (FIL•uh•ment) *n.* a very thin wire or thread. Tungsten filaments are often used in light bulbs.

n. a long thin cell or series of attached cells.

filter (FIL•ter) *n.* a device used to separate one material from others by holding it back while the others pass through.

Filtering grains from coffee

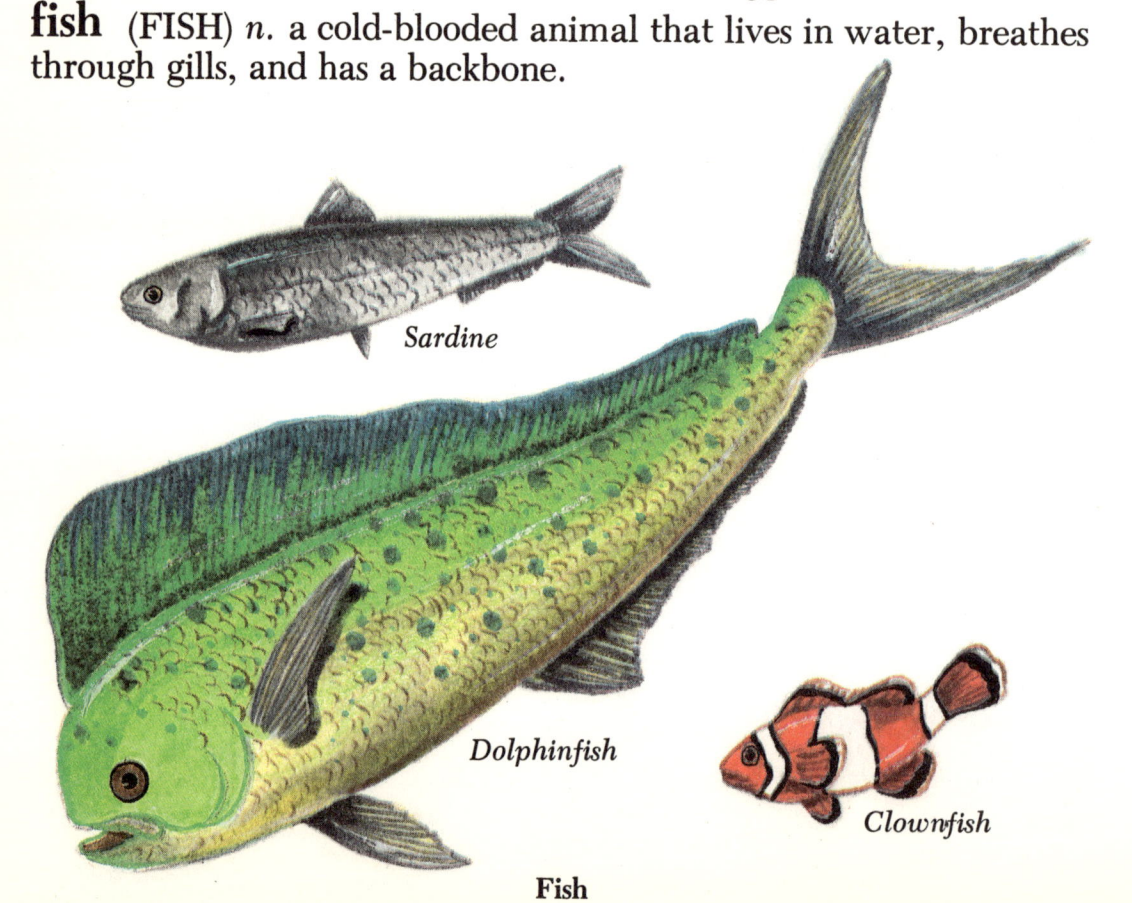

fish (FISH) *n.* a cold-blooded animal that lives in water, breathes through gills, and has a backbone.

Sardine

Dolphinfish

Clownfish

Fish

34

fission (FIZH•un) *n.* reproduction in which the parent cell divides and creates two identical cells.

n. a reaction in which the nucleus of an atom splits into new pieces and releases energy in the process.

fit (FIT) *adj.* to be in the proper condition to survive in a particular environment. Camels are fit for survival in the desert.

Dromedary camel   *Bactrian camel*

floodplains (FLUD•playnz) *n.* flat areas extending from the banks of a river which are often flooded. They are layered with sediment deposited by the river when it floods.

flora (FLOR•uh) *n.* the types of plants that live in a particular area.

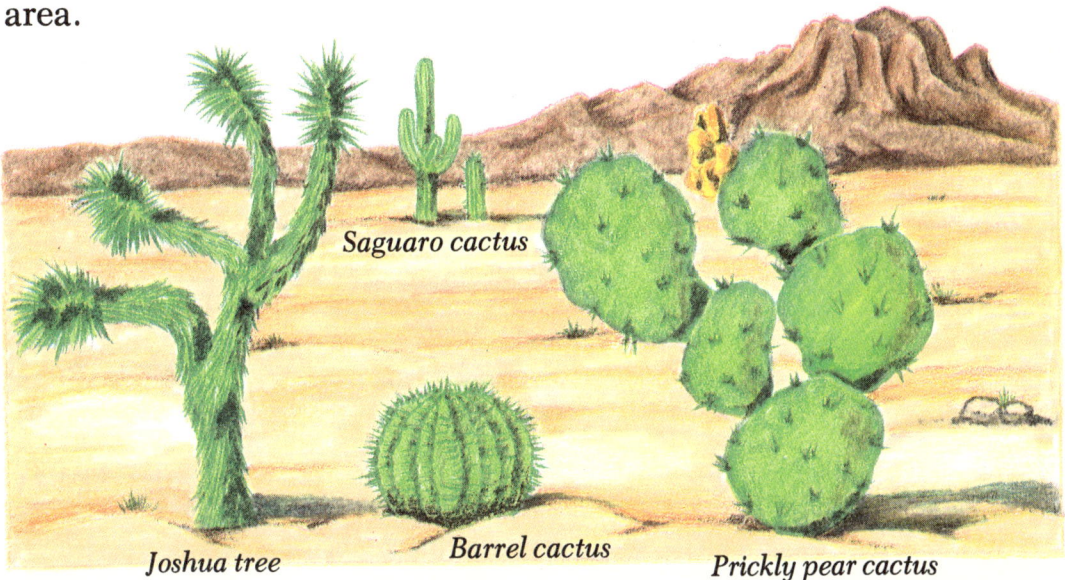

Saguaro cactus

Joshua tree   *Barrel cactus*   *Prickly pear cactus*

Plants of the desert

35

flower (FLOW·er) *n.* the part of a plant that contains the reproductive organs and produces seeds.

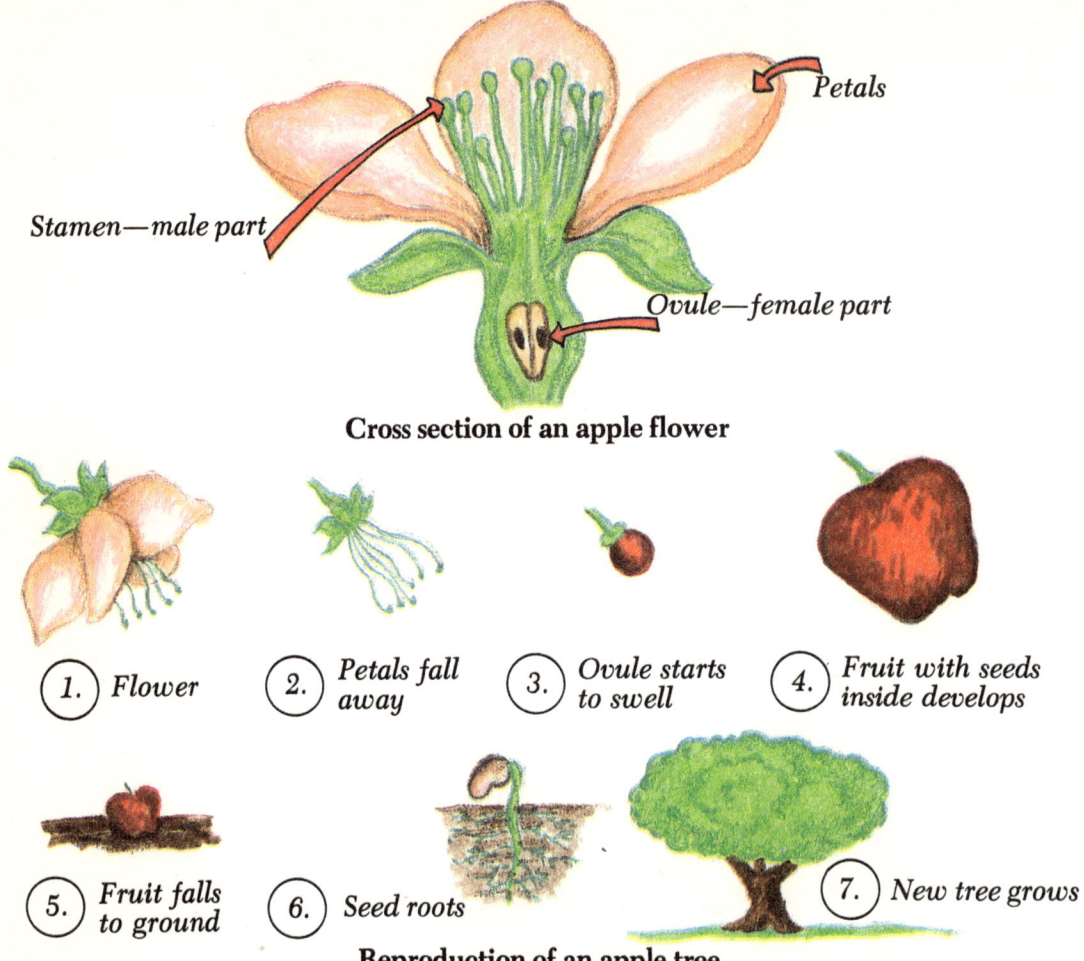

Petals

Stamen—male part

Ovule—female part

Cross section of an apple flower

1. Flower
2. Petals fall away
3. Ovule starts to swell
4. Fruit with seeds inside develops
5. Fruit falls to ground
6. Seed roots
7. New tree grows

Reproduction of an apple tree

fluid (FLOO·id) *n.* a substance that consists of particles that can move freely among themselves. Fluids take the shape of the container holding them, such as water in a glass. Fluids are not necessarily liquid.

fluorescence (flor·ESS·enss) *n.* visible light produced when certain substances absorb invisible, usually ultraviolet, light.

focus (FOH·kus) *n.* the point at which light rays appear to converge.

v. to bring together light rays to form a sharp image.

fog (FOG) *n.* a cloudlike, ground-level mass caused by water vapor condensing on dust and soot particles in the atmosphere.

fold (FOLD) *n.* a bend in the earth's crust in which layers of rock are pushed up in waves.

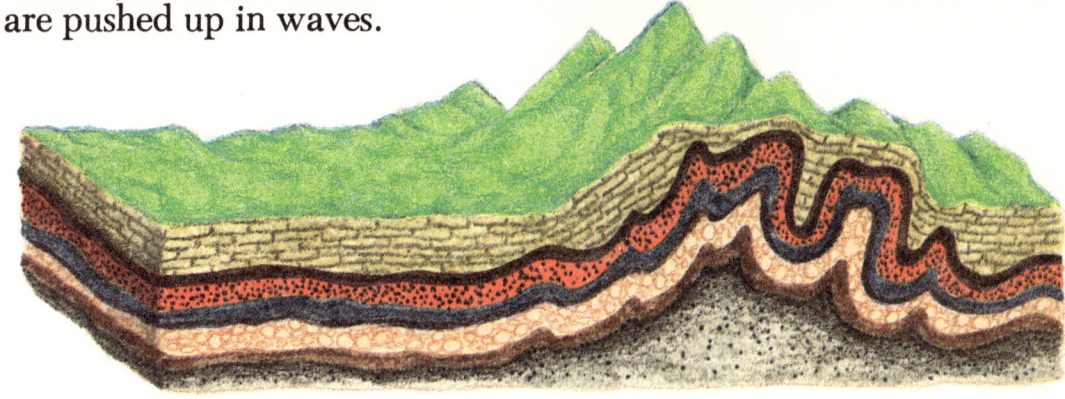

Cross section of fold mountains

follicle (FOL·ih·kul) *n.* a small open sac found in the skin and ovaries of certain animals.

n. a part of the seed capsule in plants.

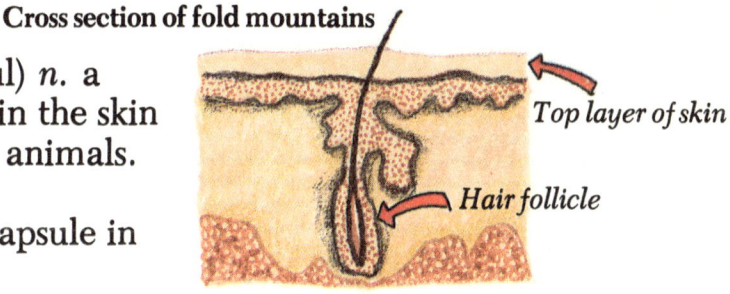

Top layer of skin

Hair follicle

Human skin

food (FOOD) *n.* a substance consumed by plants and animals for energy and nutrients such as vitamins.

food chain (FOOD CHAYN) *n.* a series of living things, beginning with plants, which are used as food by the next living thing in the chain. For example, insects eat the leaves of plants, birds eat insects, some reptiles eat birds, and certain mammals eat reptiles.

1. *Caterpillar eats leaf*
2. *Bird eats caterpillar*
3. *Snake eats bird*
4. *Lynx eats snake*

37

force (FORSS) *n.* energy or power that is exerted on an object, which tends to change the object's shape or velocity.

forecast (FOR•kast) *v.* to predict a future event, such as weather.

forest (FOR•est) *n.* an area naturally covered with many trees and often with thick undergrowth.

Forest alongside a river

fossil (FAH•sil) *n.* the remains, impressions, or other evidence of an animal or plant that lived long ago. Fossils can be bones or shells whose substance has changed to mineral. A fossil fuel, such as coal or oil, comes from the remains of prehistoric organisms.

Fossil of an Allosaurus

fraction (FRAK•shun) *n.* part of a whole number. The ratio of one number to another, usually expressed as $\frac{a}{b}$, a fraction in which *a* is called the numerator and *b* is called the denominator.

Franklin, Benjamin (FRAN•klin, BEN•juh•min) *1706–1790* An American scientist as well as a famous colonial statesman and writer. He studied electricity by flying a kite attached to a key in a lightning storm. He proved that lightning is a spark of electricity, and he developed the lightning rod, among other inventions.

freezing point (FREEZ·ing POYNT) *n.* the temperature at which a liquid becomes a solid. Water freezes at 32° Fahrenheit or 0° centigrade.

friction (FRIK·shun) *n.* resistance to the motion of one surface relative to another, such as during sliding or rolling. Friction slows motion and causes heat and wear.

front (FRUNT) *n.* the boundary between different air masses in the atmosphere.

fruit (FROOT) *n.* the part of a plant that contains and protects seeds.

Sugarpea seeds

Strawberry seeds

Acorns—oak tree seeds

Apple seeds

Fruits

fuel (FEWL) *n.* a substance that can be converted to energy.

fulcrum (FUL·krum) *n.* the point at which a lever rotates.

full moon (FULL MOON) *n.* the phase of the moon in which the entire surface facing the observer is lit by the rays of the sun.

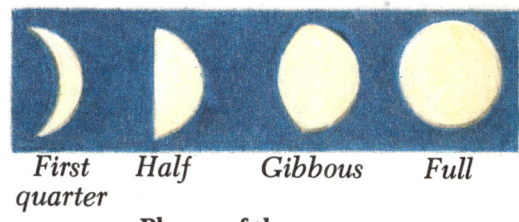

First quarter *Half* *Gibbous* *Full*

Phases of the moon

fumarole (FEW·muh·rohl) *n.* an opening in the ground in a volcanic area from which hot gases escape.

fungus (FUN·gus) *n.* plant-like living things that have no chlorophyll and cannot produce their own food. Yeast and mushrooms are fungi (plural of *fungus*).

Puffball

Mushrooms

39

fusion (FEW•zhun) *n.* when two or more substances join together to form a new substance. In nuclear fusion, atoms join together under heat and pressure to form a larger atom and generate energy. In the process, the atoms form a different kind of atom. Fusion is the source of energy in stars and the hydrogen bomb.

Gg

galaxy (GAL•ak•see) *n.* a huge group of stars revolving around a central point and moving together through space.

Spiral   *Irregular*
Two types of galaxies

Galen (GAY•len) *130?–200? A.D.* A Greek physician who established the foundations of medicine. Galen was the first person to use experiments on animals to find answers to medical questions. He discovered the presence of blood in the arteries and the function of the respiratory muscles, and proposed that the heart was responsible for causing blood to move through the body.

Galilei, Galileo (gal•ih•LAY•ee, gal•ih•LAY•oh) *1564–1642* Italian scientist Galileo made many important contributions to science. He used the newly invented telescope to chart mountains on the moon, observe the phases of Venus, and discover the four largest moons of Jupiter. Through his observations Galileo proved that the earth revolves around the sun. Galileo's study of motion served as the basis for many important theories in physics and mechanics.

gamma ray (GAA•muh RAY) *n.* a highly energetic form of electromagnetic radiation with a very short wavelength and a high frequency. Gamma rays are dangerous to living things.

gas (GAS) *n.* a form of matter which has no natural shape. The molecules are widely separated and move randomly. It takes the shape of the container that holds it.

gauge (GAYJ) *v.* to determine size, width, thickness, or degree.

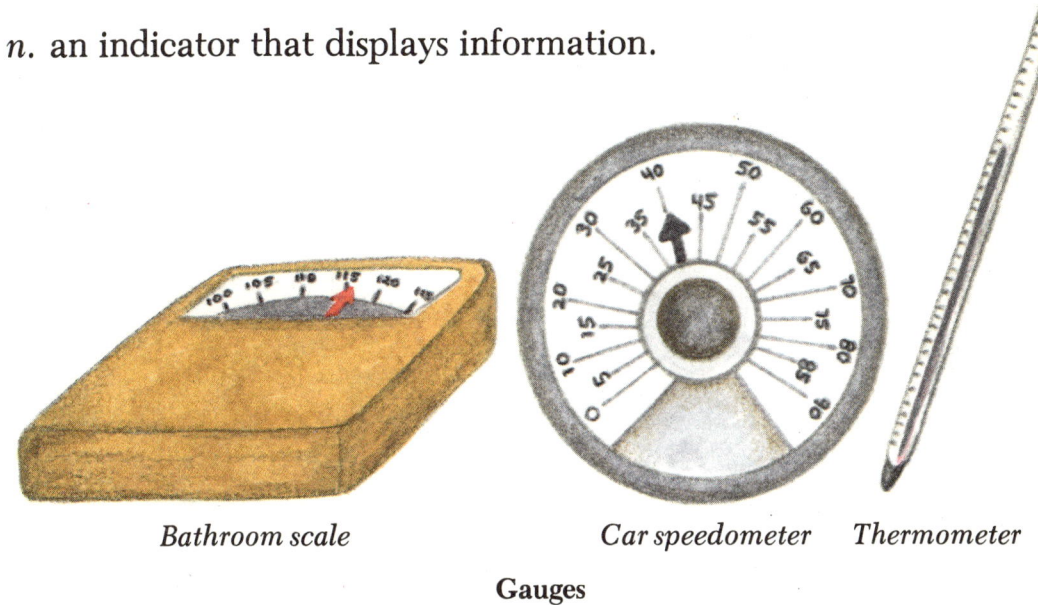

n. an indicator that displays information.

Bathroom scale   *Car speedometer*   *Thermometer*

Gauges

gene (JEEN) *n.* the part of a chromosome that controls an inherited characteristic.

generation (jen•uh•RAY•shun) *n.* an entire group of people born around the same time; the average period of time between parents and their offspring. Parents form one generation, and their offspring the next.

generator (JEN•uh•ray•ter) *n.* a machine that changes other forms of energy into electrical energy.

geology (jee•OL•oh•jee) *n.* the study of the earth's crust and reactions within it.

germinate (JER•mih•nayt) *v.* to begin to develop and grow. The activation of a seed or spore begins the growth of a new plant.

gestation (jes•TAY•shun) *n.* the period of embryo development that begins with fertilization and ends with birth. In humans the gestation period is about nine months.

geyser (GUY•zer) *n.* a hot spring that shoots a fountain of hot water and steam up through a hole in the ground. Geysers can be found in volcanic areas.

Gilbert, William (GIL•bert, WILL•yum) *1540–1603* British scientist known as the father of modern electricity. Gilbert was the first to note the difference between magnetism and static electricity. In his famous work, *De Magnete,* he described the earth as a huge magnet with a magnetic field, which he called the "Sphere of Influence."

gills (GILLZ) *n.* the organs in fish and young amphibians that allow them to take oxygen directly from water in order to breathe.

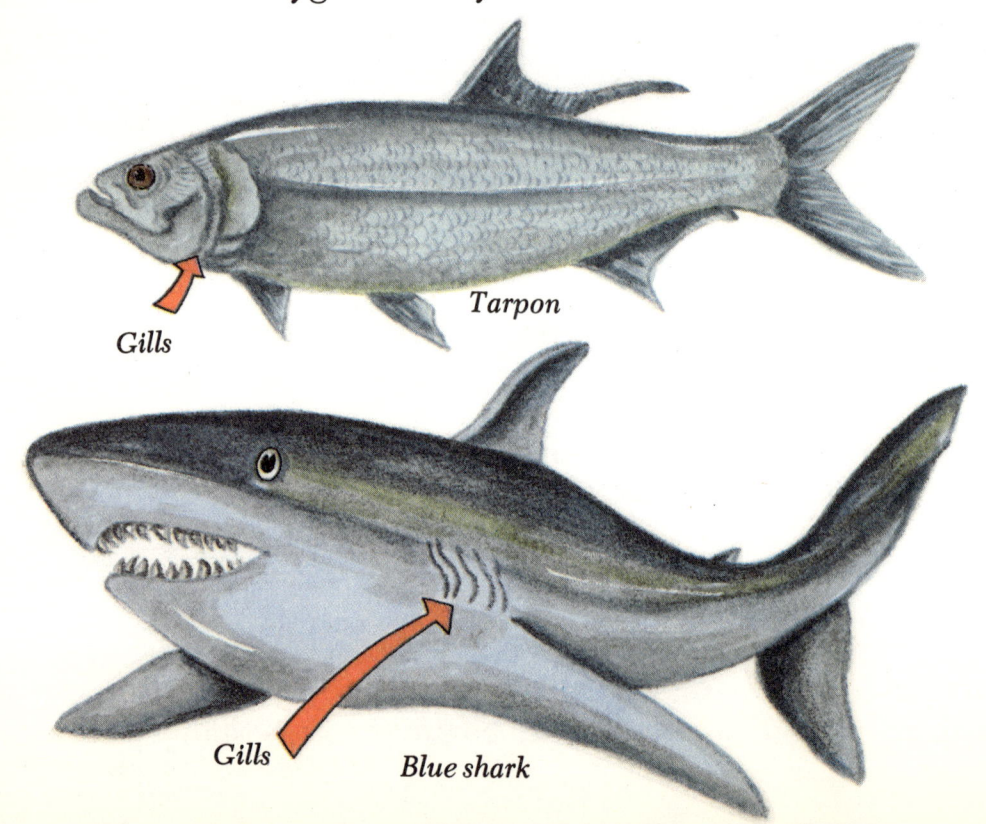

Gills
Tarpon

Gills *Blue shark*

glacier (GLAY·sher) *n.* a huge mass of ice composed largely of compressed snow that has fallen over many years. Glaciers move slowly downhill, often cutting or enlarging valleys.

Glacier enlarging a valley

gland (GLAND) *n.* a part of a living thing that produces substances either secreted or used by the body. A tear gland produces tears; a sweat gland produces sweat.

glass (GLASS) *n.* a hard, brittle substance, natural or man-made, that is often transparent. Common glass is made by combining sand, lime, and sodium carbonate. Some glass may contain lead or other metals.

glucose (GLOO·kohss) *n.* a simple sugar in blood important for many bodily functions. Glucose is produced by plants during the food-making process.

gram (GRAM) *n.* the basic unit of weight in the metric system. There are about 454 grams in one pound. There are 1,000 grams in a kilogram.

graph (GRAF) *n.* a chart that shows the relationship between two or more factors as they change.

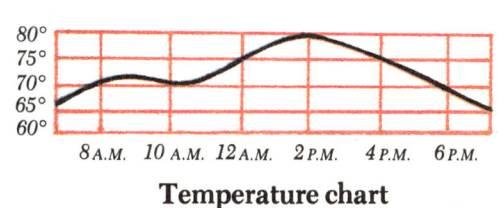

Temperature chart

gravity (GRAV·ih·tee) *n.* the force that attracts objects in space to one another. The force of Earth's gravity is measured as weight.

greenhouse effect (GREEN·howss ih·FEKT) *n.* the heating effect on the earth caused by the trapping in its atmosphere of heat radiated from the earth's surface. Excess carbon dioxide and other gases form a layer in the atmosphere that traps the heat. The greenhouse effect is a major problem today.

grid (GRID) *n.* a system of cables by which electrical power is distributed throughout an area.

n. a network of lines that form equal sections on a map to make it easier to locate an area on that map.

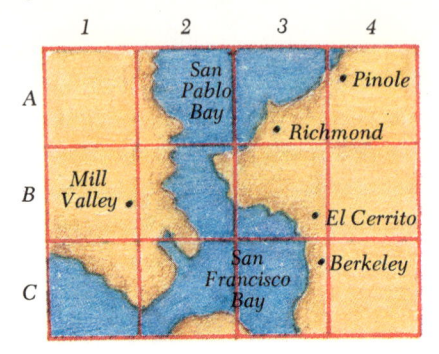

groundwater (GROWND·wat·er) *n.* water found beneath the surface of the earth.

guyot (GUY·oht) *n.* an extinct, flat-topped volcano found underwater in the ocean.

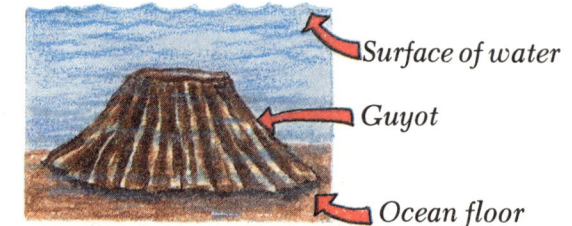

gyres (JY·erz) *n.* huge, circular motions or paths. The ocean current systems are gyres.

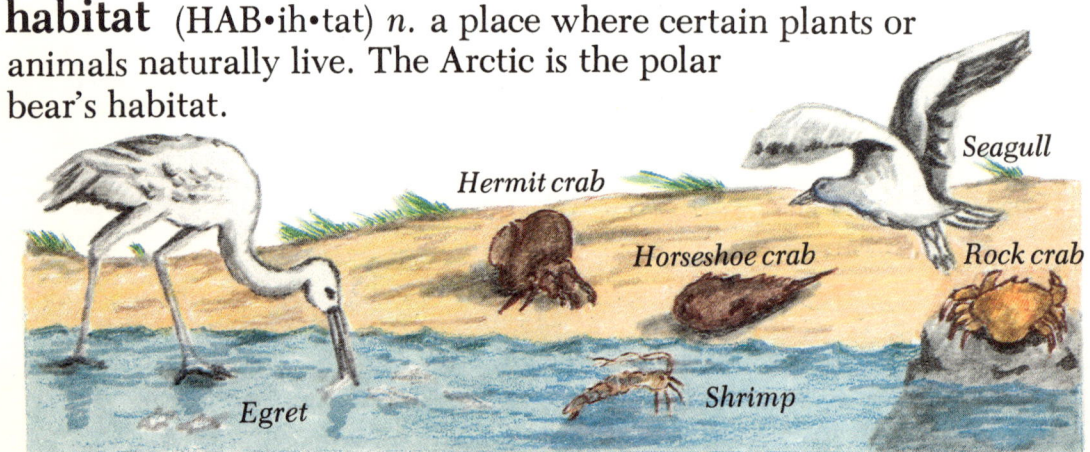

Hh

habitat (HAB·ih·tat) *n.* a place where certain plants or animals naturally live. The Arctic is the polar bear's habitat.

Animals in a marine habitat

44

hail (HAYL) *n.* small lumps of ice that fall from clouds. A piece of hail is composed of layers of ice around a dust or soot core.

hatch (HACH) *v.* to break out of an egg at birth.

Baby alligators hatching

heat (HEET) *n.* a form of energy that is released by physical and chemical processes.

hemisphere (HEM•ih•sfeer) *n.* one-half of a sphere. The equator is an imaginary line dividing the earth into the northern and southern hemispheres.

Equator

hemoglobin (HEE•moh•gloh•bin) *n.* the iron compound in red blood cells that combines easily with oxygen and gives blood its red color.

herbivore (HER•bih•vor) *n.* an animal that eats only plants. A rabbit is a herbivore.

Rabbit

heredity (her•ED•ih•tee) *n.* the passage of characteristics from one group of living organisms to their direct descendants through the genes.

Herschel, William (HER•shul, WILL•yum) *1738–1822* English astronomer who discovered the planet Uranus and binary stars—two stars that are attracted to each other by gravity. He proved that the sun is moving through space, carrying the solar system with it. He also stated that our solar system is a part of the Milky Way Galaxy.

hibernate (HY•ber•nayt) *v.* to be in an inactive state during winter. Ground squirrels and certain other animals hibernate during the winter, living on fat they have stored in their bodies. Cold-blooded animals hibernate when their body temperature drops to a certain low level.

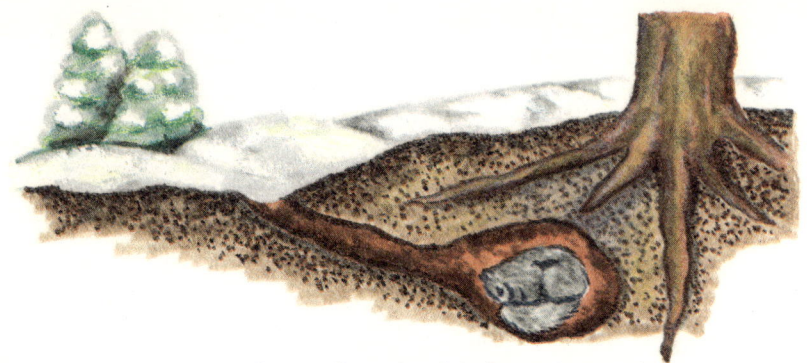

Ground squirrel in burrow

homeostasis (hoh•mee•oh•STAY•sis) *n.* the ability to maintain a constant internal environment. The internal environment includes the temperature and chemical makeup of the fluids in a living thing. Feeling thirsty and taking a drink after you have lost water by sweating is an example of homeostasis at work.

horizon (hor•EYE•zun) *n.* the point in the distance at which the earth and sky appear to meet.

Horizon line

horizontal (hor•ih•ZON•tul) *adj.* to be parallel to level ground. A table is usually made up of a horizontal surface on legs.

hormones (HOR•monz) *n.* chemical substances produced by special glands in the body. Hormones travel through the bloodstream to the part of the body in which they are needed. They affect or govern many bodily functions, such as growth and reproduction.

hot spring (HOT SPRING) *n.* a place where groundwater, heated by hot rocks, surfaces as hot water and steam.

hull (HULL) *n.* the outer covering of a nut, grain, or seed, or the small leaves around the stem of certain fruits such as strawberries.

humidity (hew·MID·ih·tee) *n.* the amount of water vapor in the air. When humidity reaches 100 percent, the water vapor may form fog.

humus (HOO·mus) *n.* a fertile substance in soil formed from decayed plants and animals.

hurricane (HER·ih·kayn) *n.* a very strong, whirling tropical storm characterized by strong winds and heavy rain revolving around a calm central core, or the eye. Hurricane winds reach more than seventy-five miles per hour, and can blow down a house.

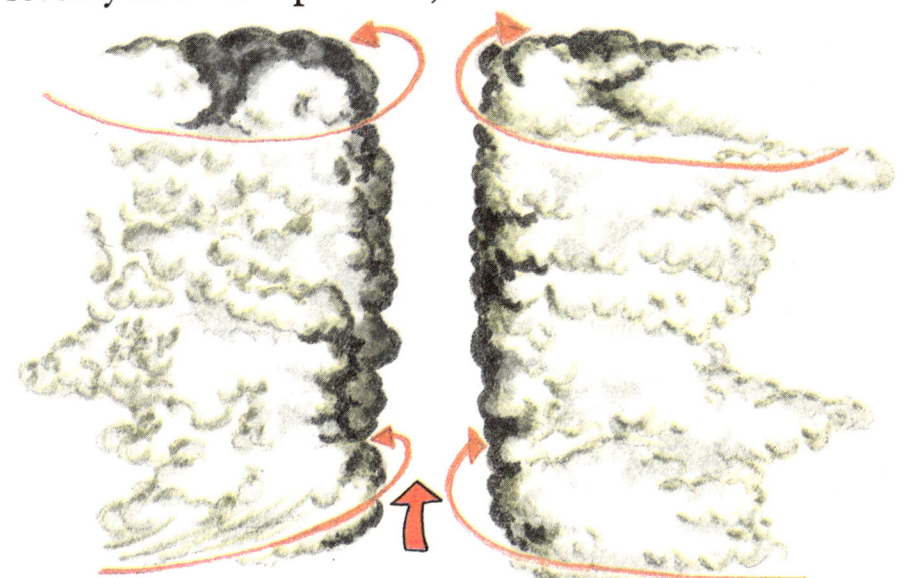

The calm eye of a hurricane

Huygens, Christian (HOY·genz, KRIS·tee·an) *1629–1695* Dutch physicist and astronomer who invented the pendulum clock. Through a telescope with powerful lenses that he ground himself, Huygens was the first person to clearly see Saturn's rings and to discover Titan, Saturn's largest moon. He did valuable work in the field of optics and stated that light travels in waves.

hydraulic (hy·DRAW·lik) *adj.* operated by force or pressure produced by moving liquids.

hydrosphere (HY·droh·sfeer) *n.* all the waters of the earth including oceans, lakes, groundwater, and rivers.

hypothesis (hy•POTH•uh•sis) *n.* a proposed explanation of how or why something happens or a possible solution to a problem. An educated guess.

n. an assumption made as part of a mathematical proof.

Ii

ice age (EYSS AYG) *n.* one of several periods on Earth when the icecaps extended much farther toward the equator and glaciers covered a great deal of the Northern Hemisphere.

The woolly mammoth lived during the Ice Age

icecap (EYSS•kap) *n.* a large, permanent mass of ice on part of a planet's surface. The earth has ice caps at the poles.

igneous (IG•nee•us) *adj.* Granite is an igneous rock, which is formed by tremendous heat or fire.

inborn (IN•born) *adj.* certain behaviors that are already in place at birth. Blinking, for example, is inborn.

incline (IN•klyn) *n.* a sloping surface.

Incline

indirect evidence (in•dy•REKT EV•ih•denss) *n.* information about how something works based on its reactions with something else. Scientists study the interior of the earth based on reactions occurring on the earth's surface.

inert (in•ERT) *adj.* having no ability to react with other substances.

inertia (in•ER•shuh) *n.* the tendency of something to keep its current state of motion whether that be at rest or moving in a straight line.

infinite (IN•fih•nit) *adj.* something that does not end or has no bounds. To be immeasurably large.

infrared (IN•fruh•red) *n.* a form of electromagnetic energy. Infrared light cannot be seen but can be felt as heat.

inorganic (in•or•GAN•ik) *adj.* referring to a substance that does not contain hydrogen and carbon. A nonliving substance.

insect (IN•sekt) *n.* an animal with three pairs of legs and a body covered with a hard outer skeleton called an exoskeleton. Its body is divided into three segments: head, thorax, and abdomen.

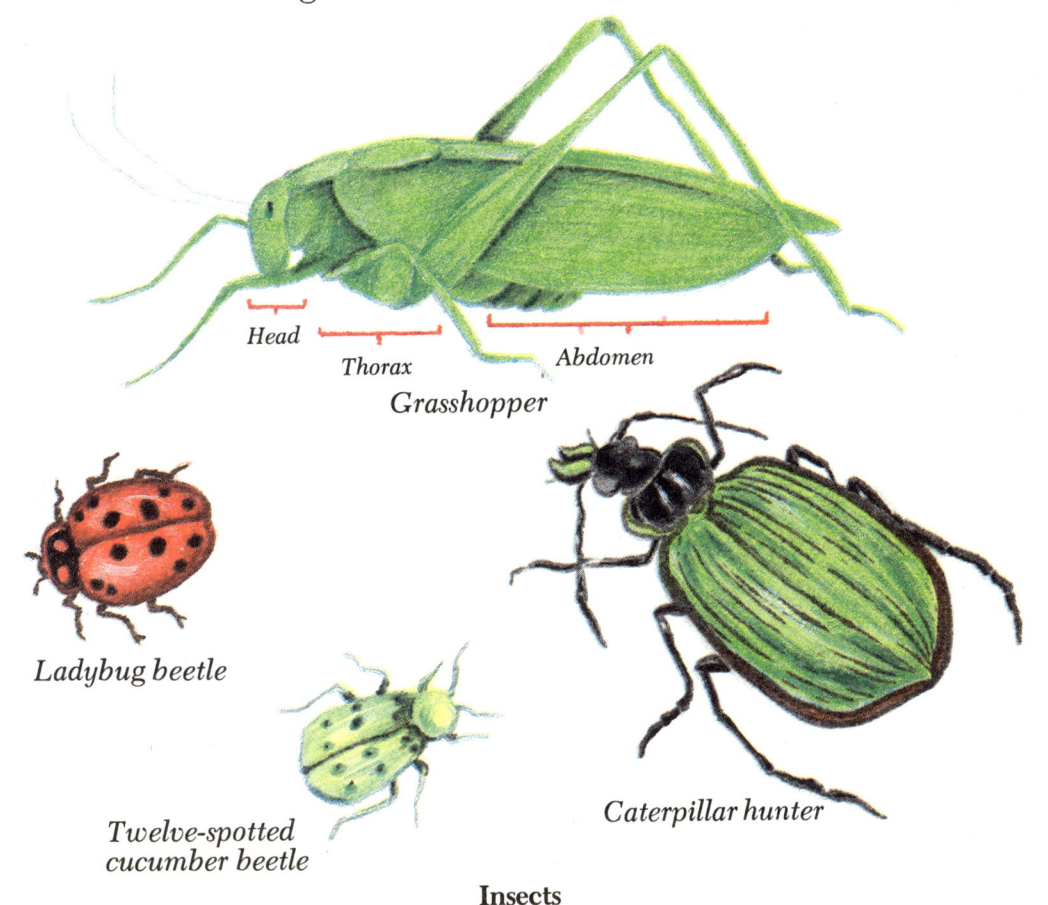

Head
Thorax
Abdomen
Grasshopper

Ladybug beetle

Twelve-spotted cucumber beetle

Caterpillar hunter

Insects

49

instrument (IN•struh•ment) *n.* a tool used to perform an experiment, or make an observation, or manipulate something.

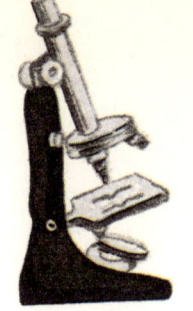

Microscope   Tweezers

insulation (in•suh•LAY•shun) *n.* a material that hinders the flow of electricity, heat, or sound. Rubber, wood, and plastics are insulators.

Electric wires covered with rubber for insulation

interstellar (in•ter•STELL•ar) *adj.* between stars in a galaxy.

intertidal (in•ter•TY•dal) *adj.* the part of a beach or shore that is between the water levels of high and low tide.

invertebrate (in•VER•tuh•brayt) *n.* an animal that does not have a backbone, such as a jellyfish.

Jellyfish   *Sea anemone*
Invertebrates

ion (EYE•on) *n.* an atom with an electrical charge, either plus (+) or minus (−), created through the loss or gain of an electron.

ionosphere (eye•ON•oh•sfeer) *n.* a layer of atmosphere that contains many electrically charged particles and stretches from 55 to 250 miles above the earth's surface.

iris (EYE•ris) *n.* the colored part of the eye, which regulates the amount of light entering through the pupil by contraction and expansion.

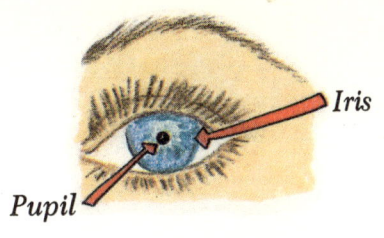

Iris
Pupil

irrigate (ER•ih•gayt) *v.* to bring water to crops other than by rainfall. Man-made irrigation makes it possible to grow crops on otherwise dry land.

island (EYE•land) *n.* a body of land surrounded by water.

An island in the ocean

isotope (EYE•soh•tohp) *n.* an atom of an element that has a different number of neutrons in its nucleus, and thus a different mass from other atoms of the same element. All isotopes of an element have the same number of protons and have the same chemical properties.

isthmus (ISS•mus) *n.* a narrow stretch of land with water on both sides that connects two larger bodies of land. The Isthmus of Panama connects North America with South America.

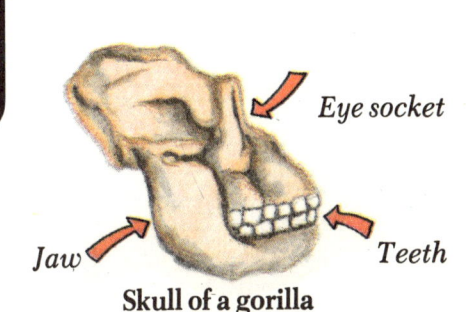

North America
Isthmus
South America

Jj

jaw (JAW) *n.* one of two bones in the skull of some animals. Jaws usually contain teeth and open and shut to obtain food.

Eye socket
Jaw
Teeth
Skull of a gorilla

51

jet stream (JET STREEM) *n.* a strong, fast-moving wind about ten miles above the earth's surface. Jet streams affect the direction of weather movements.

n. the hot gases expelled from a rocket or jet engine.

joint (JOYNT) *n.* a place where bones join. Bones have a range of movement depending on the type of joint.

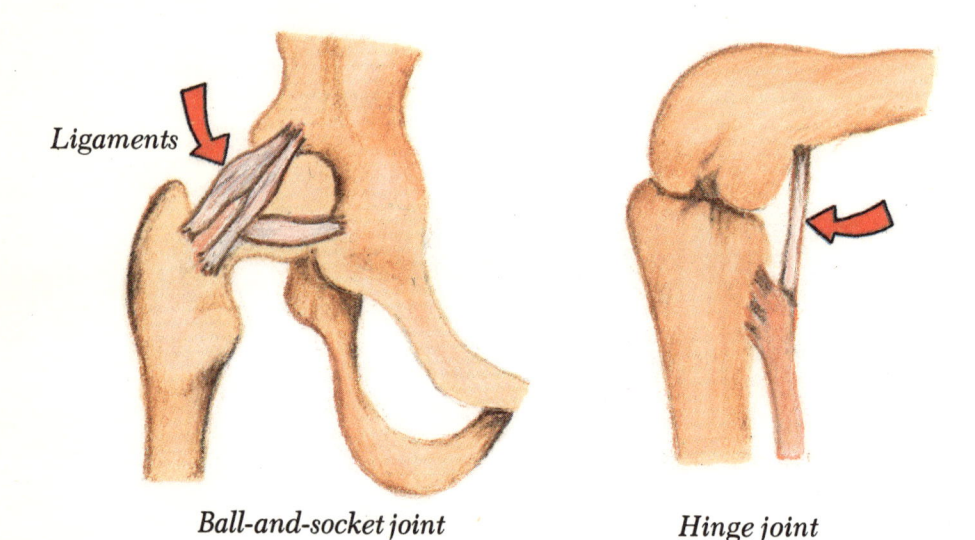

Ligaments

Ball-and-socket joint   *Hinge joint*

junction (JUNK•shun) *n.* a place where paths, such as roads or circuits, cross or join.

Kk

Kelvin (KEL•vin) *adj.* a temperature scale in which 0° is at absolute zero, the coldest possible temperature in our universe. The size of one degree Kelvin (°K) is exactly the same as one degree centigrade (°C), but 0°C is 273°K.

Kelvin, William (KEL•vin, WILL•yum) *1824–1907* English mathematician and physicist who believed that there is a temperature at which all activity stops. He called it absolute zero. This is 0° on the Kelvin temperature scale and equals −273°C. He also formulated the second law of thermodynamics, which states that when work is done some energy changes into heat.

Kepler, Johannes (KEP•ler, yoh•HAHN•us) *1571–1630* German astronomer who developed three laws that describe how planets move in space. He also stated that the tides are influenced by the gravitational pull of the moon.

kilogram (KIL•oh•gram) *n.* a unit of weight in the metric system that is equal to 1,000 grams or about 2.2 pounds.

kilometer (kih•LOM•uh•ter) *n.* a unit of length in the metric system that is equal to 1,000 meters or about 0.62 miles.

kinetic energy (kih•NET•ik EN•er•jee) *n.* the energy of movement. The faster something moves, the more kinetic energy it has.

kingdom (KING•dum) *n.* one of the three main divisions in nature—animal, plant, mineral.

Animal kingdom   *Vegetable kingdom*   *Mineral kingdom*

knot (NOT) *n.* a unit of measure of speed at sea or in the air. One knot is equal to one nautical mile per hour, which is equal to about 6,075 feet on land.

Ll

laboratory (LAB•ruh•tor•ee) *n.* a place where scientific studies, measurements, or experiments are performed.

lagoon (luh·GOON) *n.* a shallow, usually calm body of water separated from an ocean or sea by coral reefs or sandbars.

larva (LAR·vuh) *n.* the wingless, immature feeding stage which follows hatching from an egg in the life of some insects. A caterpillar is the larva of a moth or butterfly.

Larva *Cocoon* *Silk moth*

The metamorphosis of the silk moth

laser (LAY·zer) *n.* an instrument that produces a very powerful, narrow beam of light. Lasers are used in many fields including medicine, physics, and astronomy.

latitude (LAA·tih·tood) *n.* distance north or south of the equator, measured in degrees. Imaginary lines around the earth, running parallel to the equator from east to west, are used to determine latitude.

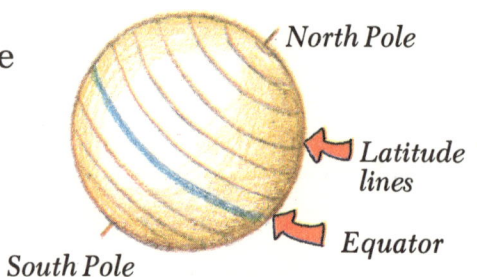

North Pole
Latitude lines
Equator
South Pole

lava (LAV·uh) *n.* molten rock from a volcano that flows down its sides or is exploded into the air.

Lava *Volcano*

law of superposition (LAW of soo•per•poh•ZIH•shun) *n.* the law of geology which states that in layers of rock, the older layers will be found at the bottom.

leach (LEECH) *v.* the removal of dissolvable materials from a solid when water or another liquid passes through it. Rainwater can leach out many important minerals as it passes through the soil.

leaf (LEEF) *n.* a part of a plant that usually contains chlorophyll, a substance that traps energy from the sun to make food for the plant.

lens (LENZ) *n.* the part of the eye that focuses light on the retina.

n. a piece of glass or transparent material that has a curved surface and can bend light rays.

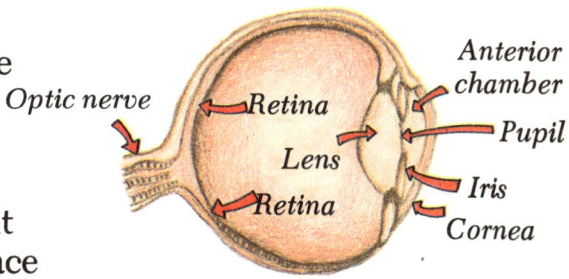

The human eye

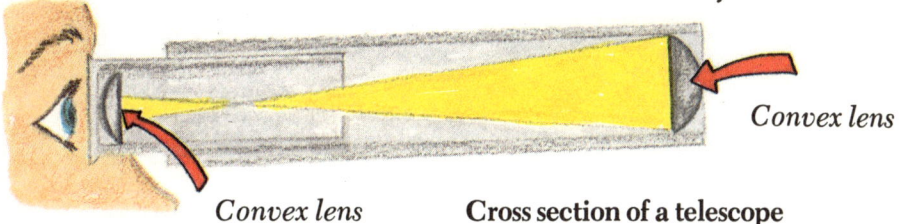

Convex lens   *Cross section of a telescope*

levee (LEV•ee) *n.* a raised bank on each side of a river. Man-made levees are often built to prevent flooding.

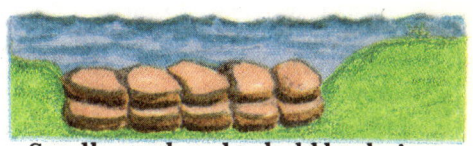

Sandbags placed to hold back river

lever (LEV•er) *n.* a simple machine that consists of a bar and a point of support. A crowbar is a lever.

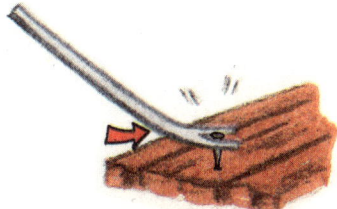

Crowbar pushes against board to remove nail

Long rod acts as lever to move large rock

lichen (LY·ken) *n.* two plants, an alga and a fungus, living together because each provides something that helps the other survive.

Fungus filaments — *Alga*

Devil's matches *Cup*

Cross section of a lichen   **Two types of lichen**

life cycle (LYF SY·kul) *n.* the changes a living thing goes through as it matures, including birth, reproduction, and death.

lift (LIFT) *n.* the force created by the difference in air pressure below and above the wings of a flying object, which enables it to stay in flight.

ligament (LIG·uh·ment) *n.* a tough band of tissue connecting bones at a joint or holding organs in place.

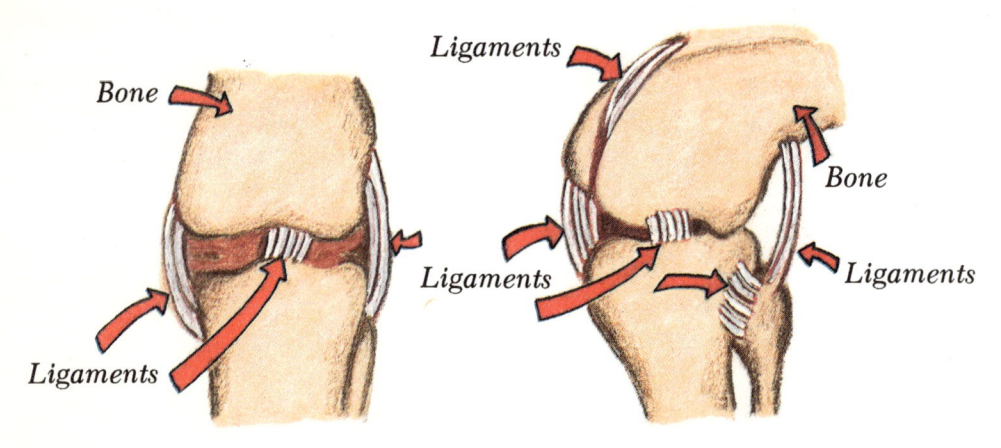

Bone *Ligaments* *Bone*
Ligaments *Ligaments* *Ligaments*

Knee joint viewed from front   **Knee joint viewed from side**

light (LYT) *n.* a form of energy that travels in waves at a speed of 186,000 miles per second. The wavelength of light determines its color.

lightning (LYT·ning) *n.* a bright flash of light produced by atmospheric electricity traveling between two electrically charged clouds or between a cloud and the ground. The earth is struck by lightning about one hundred times every second.

light-year (LYT-yeer) *n.* a measure of distance based on the distance light travels in one Earth year. One light-year is nearly six trillion (6,000,000,000,000) miles.

line (LYN) *n.* the shortest distance between two points. A geometric figure which extends in two directions without curving.

liquid (LIK·wid) *n.* a state of matter between a solid and a gas, which takes the shape of its container but does not move as freely as gas. Water is a liquid.

liter (LEE·ter) *n.* a unit of volume measurement in the metric system. A liter is equal to 1.0567 quarts. One liter of water weighs one kilogram.

lithification (lih·thih·fih·KAY·shun) *n.* the process by which loose materials such as sand and minerals are consolidated into solid rock.

lithosphere (LITH·oh·sfeer) *n.* the hard outer layer of the earth, which includes the outer crust and a part of the upper layer of the mantle. The lithosphere is approximately fifty miles (or eighty kilometers) thick.

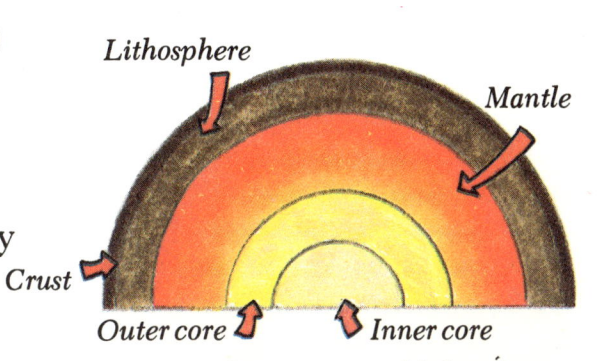

Cross section of lithosphere

57

litmus paper (LIT•mus PAY•per) *n.* a type of paper treated with a special substance that causes the paper to turn blue in a base solution, and red in an acid solution.

loam (LOHM) *n.* a rich soil composed of clay, sand, silt, and humus.

locomotion (loh•koh•MOH•shun) *n.* the act of moving from one place to another.

lodestone (LOHD•stohn) *n.* also called magnetite, a rock that contains iron and is a natural magnet. Early Chinese used lodestone as a simple compass.

North pole of magnet
Lodestone
Pieces of lodestone

logarithmic scale (log•uh•RITH•mik SKAYL) *n.* a scale in which an increase of one unit corresponds to an actual increase ten times greater. The Richter scale, used to measure earthquakes, is logarithmic. A quake measuring two on the scale is ten times stronger than a quake that measures one.

longitude (LON•jih•tood) *n.* distance east or west of the prime meridian (in Greenwich, England), measured in degrees. Imaginary lines called longitude lines or meridians, which run from the North Pole to the South Pole, are used to determine longitude.

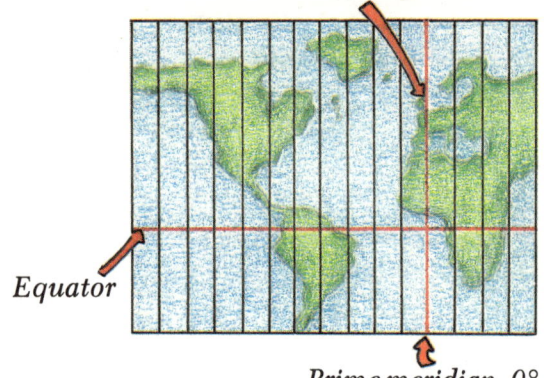

Greenwich, England
Equator
Prime meridian, 0°

lubricant (LOO•brih•kant) *n.* a substance used to reduce friction between moving parts by allowing them to slip past each other more easily. Oil is a lubricant when applied to metal parts that move against each other.

lunar (LOO•nar) *adj.* having to do with the moon.

lungs (LUNGZ) *n.* the organs certain air-breathing animals use to absorb oxygen and release carbon dioxide from the body.

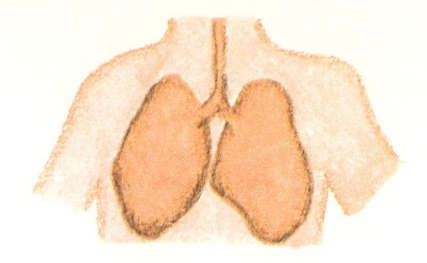

Mm

Mach (MAHK) *n.* the ratio of the speed of something compared with the speed of sound. Airplanes flying at Mach 1 are flying at exactly the speed of sound. Speeds greater than Mach 1 are faster than the speed of sound and are called supersonic.

magma (MAG•muh) *n.* molten rock material beneath the earth's crust. During volcanic eruptions magma is forced to the surface.

Reservoir of molten magma

magnet (MAG•net) *n.* an object that can attract iron or steel and is surrounded by an area of force called a magnetic field. Earth is a magnet.

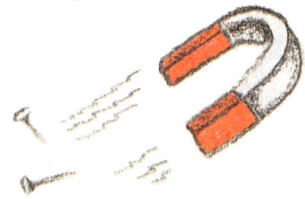

magnetosphere (mag•NET•oh•sfeer) *n.* the region surrounding a planet or star, which includes any magnetic field produced by that body.

mammal (MAM•ul) *n.* a warm-blooded animal that produces milk to feed its young and has a backbone, and hair or fur.

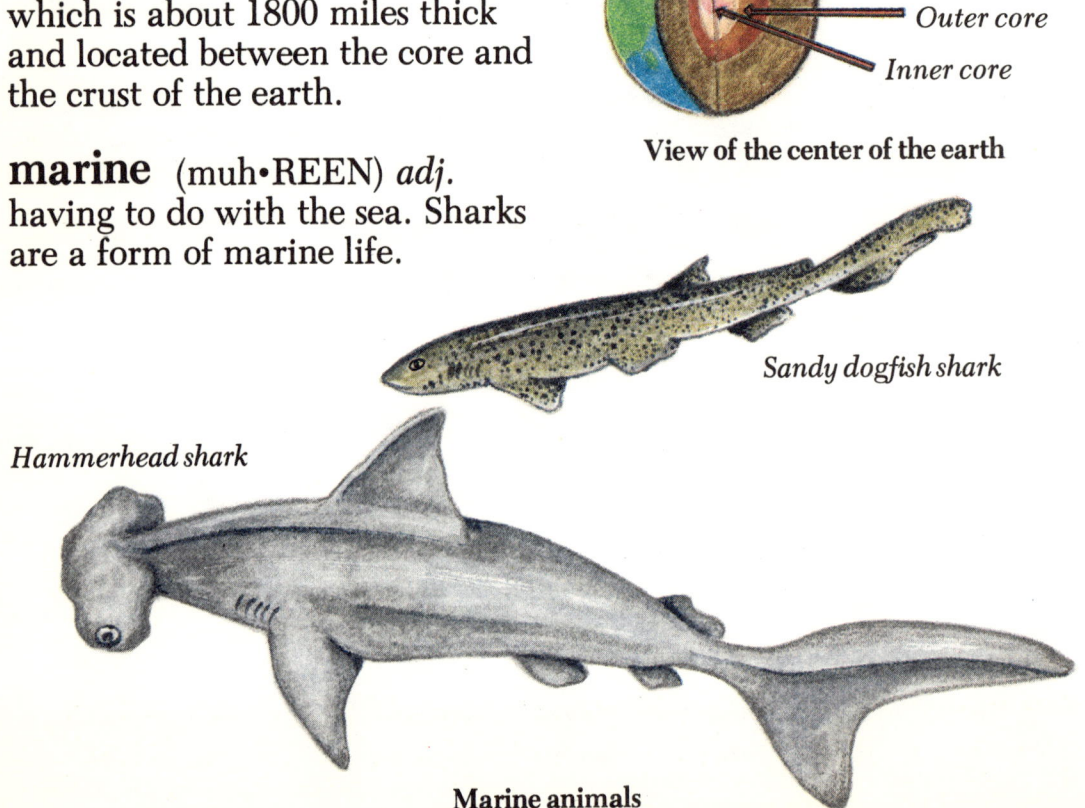

Russet mouse lemur

South American sea lion

Mountain goat

Mammals

mantle (MAN•tul) *n.* a layer of hot, sometimes molten rock, which is about 1800 miles thick and located between the core and the crust of the earth.

Crust
Mantle
Outer core
Inner core

View of the center of the earth

marine (muh•REEN) *adj.* having to do with the sea. Sharks are a form of marine life.

Sandy dogfish shark

Hammerhead shark

Marine animals

60

marrow (MAYR·oh) *n.* living tissue in the middle of most bones. Blood cells are produced in the marrow of bones.

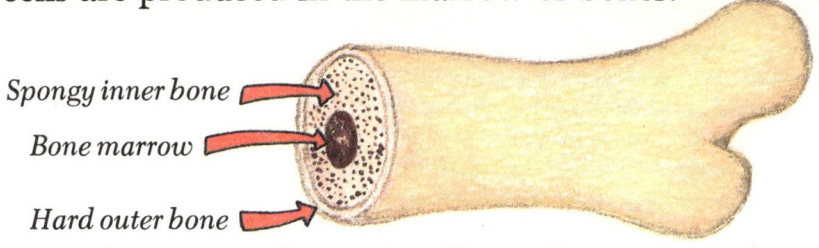

Spongy inner bone
Bone marrow
Hard outer bone

Cross section of human bone

marsupial (mar·SOO·pee·ul) *n.* a type of mammal whose young are almost always carried in a pouch on the mother's abdomen. Kangaroos and opossums are marsupials.

Koala

Short-tailed opossum

Kangaroo

Marsupials

mass (MASS) *n.* the amount of matter in a substance.

mathematics (math·uh·MAT·iks) *n.* the study of numbers, shapes, and quantities and how they relate to one another. The relationships are often expressed as equations. There are many different kinds of mathematics, including algebra, geometry, and calculus.

61

matrix (MAY•triks) *n.* an underlying framework or structure in a substance. In composite substances, such as living tissues and certain rocks, one type of substance is embedded in a matrix made of a second type of substance. Fossils are often found embedded in a matrix of stone.

Leaf fossil

matter (MATT•er) *n.* any material that has weight and takes up space. The most important building blocks of matter are protons, neutrons, and electrons.

meander (mee•AN•der) *n.* a bend in the course of a river.

Aerial view of a river

mechanics (mih•KAN•iks) *n.* the study of the behavior of physical objects when acted on by one or more forces. For example, laws of mechanics can be used to predict the action of a lever, a pulley, or a falling object.

medium (MEE•dee•um) *n.* any material used to grow microorganisms in a laboratory.

adj. average or midway between two extremes, such as large and small.

medulla (meh•DOO•lah) *n.* a part of the brain stem at the beginning of the spinal cord that controls the automatic activities of the body, such as breathing and digestion.

Medulla

melt (MELT) *v.* to change from a solid to a liquid.

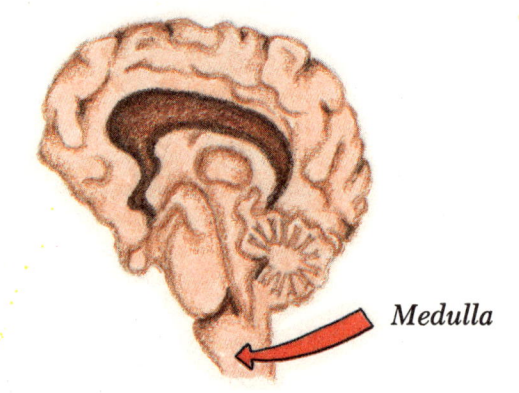

membrane (MEM•brayn) *n.* a layer made mostly of fat that surrounds, separates, and protects all living cells. Certain organs, such as the lungs, kidneys, and heart, are also contained within membranes.

Mendel, Gregor (MEN•dul, GREH•gor) *1822–1884* Austrian monk who studied heredity in plants. He noted that though two traits may be inherited by the same plant, one may be visible (dominant) and one not (recessive). For example, if red is a dominant trait, a red and white flower will probably produce a red flower, not a pink or white one.

metabolism (muh•TAB•oh•liz•um) *n.* the physical and chemical changes in the body that release energy as food is used.

metal (MET•ul) *n.* a mineral substance that can conduct heat and electricity. Under normal conditions most metals are solid. Gold, silver, and copper are all metals.

metamorphic (met•uh•MOR•fik) *adj.* rocks such as marble that have changed form due to extreme heat and pressure.

Black marble   *Quartzite*   *Eclogite*

metamorphosis (met•uh•MOR•fuh•sis) *n.* a profound change from one state to another in the life cycle of an organism. For example, a butterfly is first a caterpillar, then a pupa, before assuming its final, adult form.

meteoroid (MEE•tee•uh•royd) *n.* a relatively small body that travels through space. When a meteoroid enters the earth's atmosphere, it can be seen as a streak of light called a meteor. If it hits the earth's surface it becomes a meteorite.

Meteor that has entered Earth's atmosphere

63

meteorology (mee•tee•uh•ROL•oh•jee) *n.* the study of the earth's atmosphere, including the conditions that cause all types of weather.

meter (MEE•ter) *n.* a unit of measure of length in the metric system. One meter measures 39.4 inches, or slightly more than one yard.

n. a device used to measure the amount of something.

metric system (MEH•trik SIS•tem) *n.* a system of scientific measurement, based on units of ten. The basic unit of *length* is the meter, of *volume* the liter, and of *weight* the gram. The prefix kilo, as in kilometer, added to any of these units means 1,000 times more. The prefix centi means one one-hundredth ($\frac{1}{100}$) and milli is one one-thousandth ($\frac{1}{1,000}$). In the metric system temperature is measured in degrees centigrade or Celsius (°C).

microorganism (MY•kroh•OR•guh•niz•um) *n.* a living thing too small to be seen without a microscope. A virus is a microorganism.

microscope (MY•kroh•skohp) *n.* a scientific instrument with a system of lenses used to focus on small objects and magnify them so that they can be seen in greater detail. Light microscopes focus beams of visible light, and electron microscopes focus beams of electrons.

Cross section of a light microscope

midocean ridge (MID•oh•shun RIJ) *n.* an undersea mountain range that winds for more than 30,000 miles under the oceans. New ocean floor is produced at midocean ridges by molten rock rising up through cracks in a ridge.

Midocean ridges

migrate (MY•grayt) *v.* to travel great distances from one place to another and usually back again. Birds migrate south for the winter. The American golden plover migrates each year from Alaska to Hawaii.

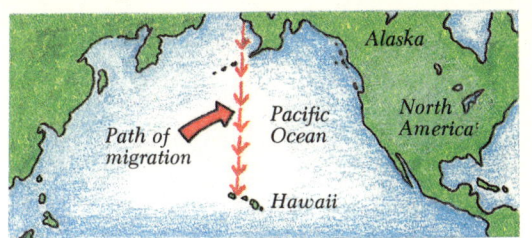

Milky Way (MIL•kee WAY) *n.* the galaxy in which our solar system is contained.

mineral (MIN•er•ul) *n.* a natural element or compound, almost always inorganic, with a certain chemical composition and often a certain crystal structure.

Gold crystal   Gold ore

mirage (mih•RAZH) *n.* an image of an object that appears to be at some location other than its true position. It is caused by the bending or reflection of light rays in a certain way in the atmosphere. Mirages usually occur at sea or in the desert.

mixture (MIKS•cher) *n.* a combination of two or more materials or substances.

model (MOD•ul) *n.* a small copy of an object, idea, or event that is usually used for demonstration or experimentation.

mold (MOLD) *n.* a fungus that causes organic matter to decay. It has no chlorophyll and lives on other plants or animals.

Stinkhorn

Bird's-nest fungi

Truffle

Mushroom

Fungi

n. a hollow form used to produce a copy of something by being filled with a liquid material that then hardens, taking the shape of the form.

65

molecule (MOL•uh•kewl) *n.* the simplest chemical unit. Molecules are made up of two or more atoms that bind together. One molecule of water is made of two atoms of hydrogen and one atom of oxygen (H_2O).

mollusk (MOLL•usk) *n.* a type of animal with no backbone and a soft body divided into a head and a foot. Many, such as clams, have a hard protective shell. A squid is a mollusk without a shell.

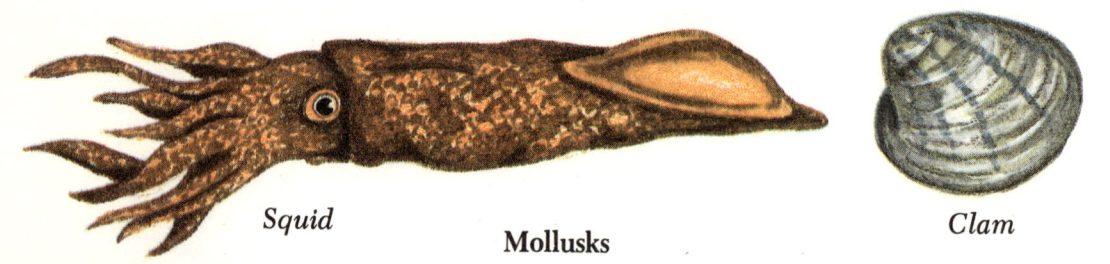

Squid *Clam*
Mollusks

momentum (moh•MEN•tum) *n.* the force produced by a moving body. Momentum tends to keep an object moving in the same direction at the same speed.

month (MUNTH) *n.* a unit of time which is approximately equal to the time it takes the moon to make one complete circle around the earth. A month is thirty or thirty-one days long. February has twenty-eight days, except during leap year, when it gains one day.

moon (MOON) *n.* a body in space which travels in orbit around a planet. Earth has one moon. Jupiter has sixteen.

Earth

Moon in orbit around Earth    Cratered surface of Earth's moon

moraine (mor•AYN) *n.* large amounts of rock and soil that have been pushed up along the side or in front of a moving glacier.

mucus (MEW•kus) *n.* a thick fluid produced by the glands of the body to lubricate, moisten, and protect surfaces. In many mammals, mucus lines the mouth, nose, air passages, and intestines. The trails left by snails and slugs are made of mucus.

multicellular (mul•tee•SELL•yew•lar) *adj.* describes a living thing made up of many cells.

muscle (MUS•ul) *n.* tissue composed of cells that cause movement when they contract. There are three types of muscles in humans: cardiac muscle in the heart, smooth muscle in the organs and intestines, and skeletal muscle attached to the bones.

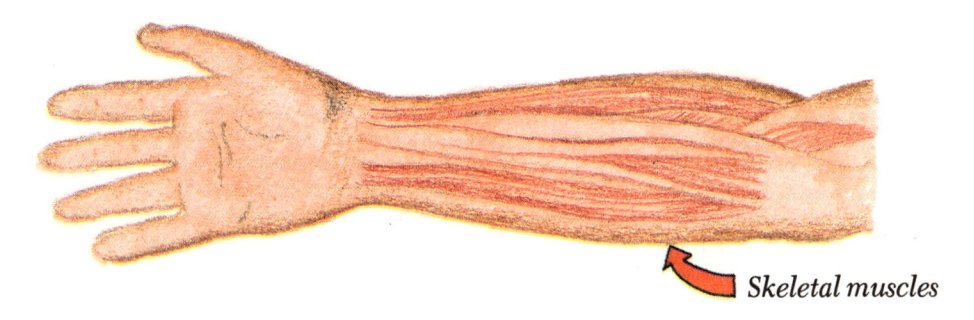

Skeletal muscles

Bending muscles for wrist and hand

mutation (mew•TAY•shun) *n.* a change in the genes of a living thing that may cause a change in the characteristics of its offspring.

Nn

natural gas (NACH•uh•rul GAS) *n.* a gas often found with oil deposits and used as a fuel.

natural selection (NACH•uh•rul suh•LEK•shun) *n.* the theory which states that the organisms best adapted to a particular environment will survive more easily and produce more offspring than other, less well suited organisms.

navigation (nav•uh•GAY•shun) *n.* the science of locating one's position on land, on sea, or in the air, and directing a course to another position.

neap tide (NEEP TYD) *n.* the tide that occurs twice each month and during which there is only a very small difference between the water levels of high and low tides.

nebula (NEB•yew•luh) *n.* a cloud of dust and gas in space.

nectar (NEK•tar) *n.* a sweet liquid produced by some flowers and used as food by insects and birds that pollinate the flowers.

Hummingbird sipping nectar at base of flower

nerve (NERV) *n.* a bundle of fibers that receive, process, and send information to and from the brain or spinal cord and other parts of the body.

nervous system (NER•vus SIS•tem) *n.* the network of nerves and organs in man and animals that senses the environment and controls bodily functions.

neuron (NEWR•on) *n.* a type of nerve cell—made up of a cell body, axon, and nerve ending—that transmits messages between the brain and other parts of the body.

Cell body   *Axon*   Neuron

neutral (NOO•trul) *adj.* having characteristics midway between acid and base, or describing a substance that has neither a positive nor negative charge.

neutron (NOO•tron) *n.* a small particle having no charge, usually found together with protons in the nucleus of an atom.

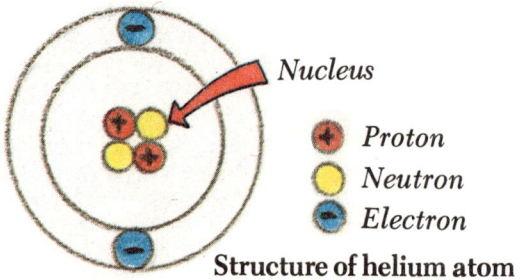

Nucleus
+ *Proton*
Neutron
− *Electron*

Structure of helium atom

neutron star (NOO•tron STAR) *n.* a very small, dense spinning star that is all that remains after the supernova of a red supergiant star.

new moon (NOO MOON) *n.* the phase of the moon in which it appears as only a very thin crescent shape or is invisible.

Newton, Isaac (NOO•tun, EYE•zak) *1642–1727* English mathematician, astronomer, physicist, and one of the world's greatest scientists. He described the nature of light—including refraction—and invented the reflecting telescope. He studied the effect of force on moving objects, the movement of fluids, and the motion of planets, but he is best known for discovering the law of gravity.

niche (NICH) *n.* a certain type of environment with characteristic types and amounts of resources to which particular plants and/or animals have become adapted.

nitrogen (NY•troh•jen) *n.* a colorless, odorless, gaseous element that makes up four-fifths of the earth's atmosphere.

nocturnal (nok•TERN•ul) *adj.* happening during the night. Bats are called nocturnal animals because they are active during the night.

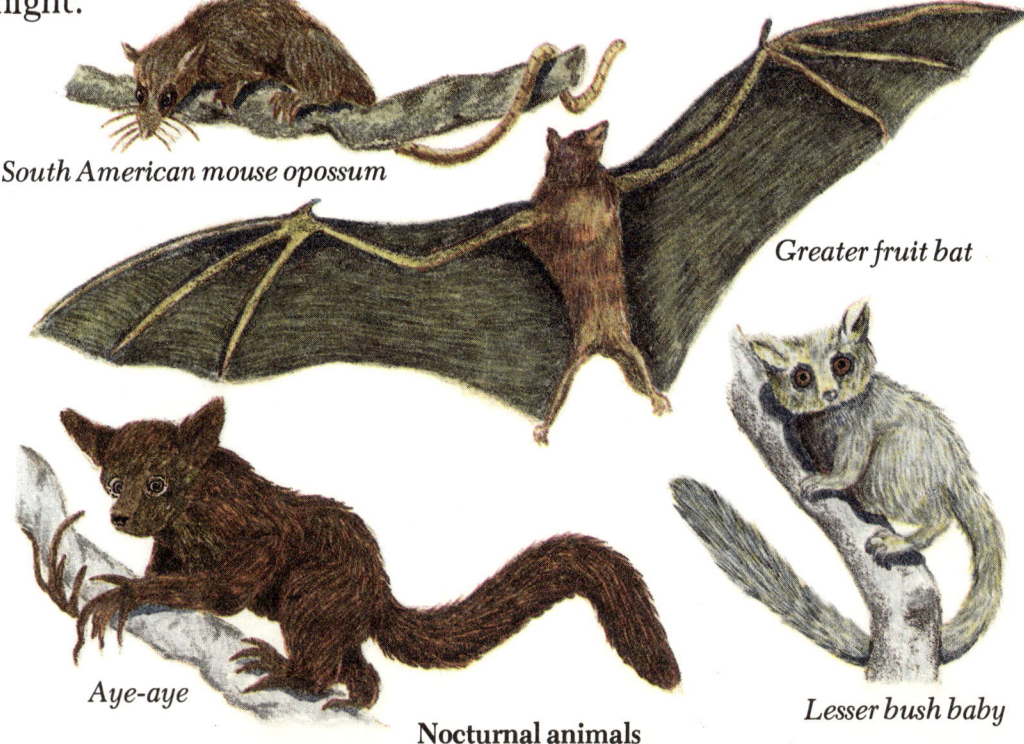

South American mouse opossum

Greater fruit bat

Aye-aye

Lesser bush baby

Nocturnal animals

69

nonrenewable (non•ree•NOO•uh•bul) *adj.* not replaceable after it has been used. Oil is a nonrenewable source of fuel.

nova (NOH•vuh) *n.* a star that suddenly flares very brightly, shining intensely for a while and then dimming back to its original brightness.

nucleus (NOO•klee•us) *n.* a membrane-enclosed area in most living cells that contains DNA and controls growth and reproduction of the cell.

Nucleus

Human cell

n. the center of an atom that contains protons and neutrons. During atomic fission the nucleus is split and a tremendous amount of energy is released.

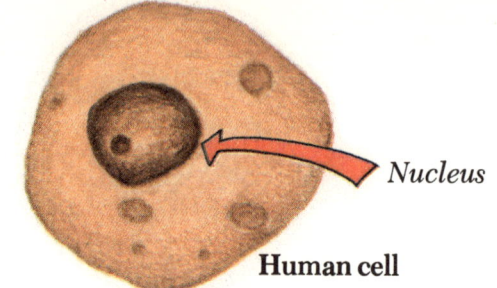

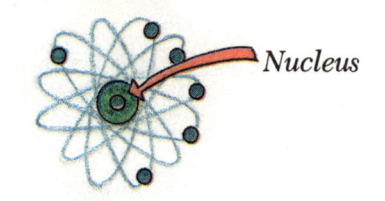

Nucleus

nutrients (NOO•tree•ents) *n.* the elements in food that the body can either convert to energy or use to build new cells.

Oo

oasis (oh•AY•sus) *n.* a place in the desert where water comes to the surface in the form of a spring or well, and the land around it is green and fertile as a result.

An oasis in the desert

occultation (ah•kul•TAY•shun) *n.* cutting off of light from a body in space when another body passes between it and the observer. A solar eclipse is an example of an occultation.

ocean (OH•shun) *n.* a large, deep body of salt water. Oceans cover three-fourths of the surface of the earth.

ocean basin (OH•shun BAY•sun) *n.* the floor; the deepest part of an ocean.

ohm (OHM) *n.* a unit used to measure resistance to the flow of electrons in a current.

omnivore (OM•nih•vor) *n.* an animal that will eat both plants and animals. Humans and some other animals are omnivores.

Human   **Omnivores**   *Raccoon*

ooze (OOZ) *n.* a thick sediment found on the plains of the ocean basin and formed by organic remains such as shells that have drifted down from the surface.

opaque (oh•PAYK) *adj.* used to describe something that does not let light pass through.

optical illusion (OP•tih•kul ih•LOO•zhun) *n.* something that is not exactly as it appears when seen.

Two horizontal lines are equal   Two red circles are equal

optics (OP•tiks) *n.* the study of the interaction of light with matter.

orbit (OR•bit) *n.* the path of an object in space that is moving around another object. The moon is in orbit around the earth.

order (OR•der) *n.* a classification of living things into a large group with a major characteristic in common. Monkeys, apes, and humans all belong to the order Primates.

ore (OR) *n.* a mineral in the earth that contains metals.

Pyrite   *Fluorite*   *Galena*
Common ores

organ (OR•gun) *n.* a part of the body that does a particular job or jobs for the purpose of helping the entire body to work properly. The heart is an organ.

organic (or•GAN•ik) *adj.* used to describe anything produced by living things.

adj. used to describe anything which contains the element carbon.

organism (OR•guh•niz•um) *n.* a living thing, plant, or animal.

osmosis (oz•MOH•sis) *n.* the movement of molecules (usually water) through a membrane that separates two solutions of different concentration. Osmosis occurs only when the solids in a solution cannot pass through the membrane dividing the two solutions. During osmosis, water always moves from the solution of lower concentration to the solution of higher concentration.

outcrop (OWT•krop) *n.* the part of a layer of rock that sticks out and is exposed to the surface.

oviparous (oh•VIP•uh•rus) *adj.* referring to animals such as chickens that produce eggs within the body but release them to be hatched.

Hen tending her eggs

ovule (AHV·yewl) *n.* the part of a flower that after being fertilized becomes a seed. It contains the egg cell.

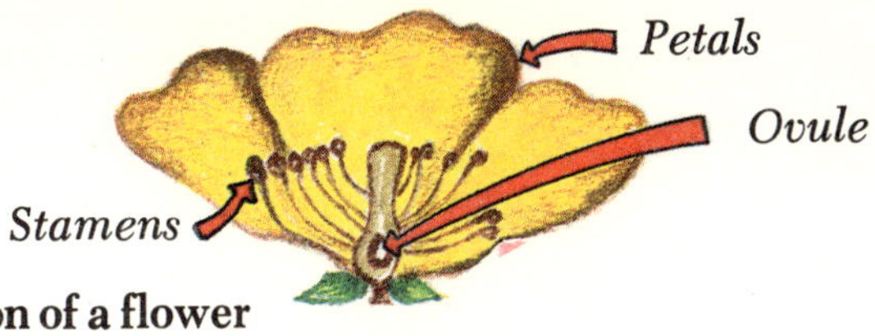

Cross section of a flower

oxidation (oks·ih·DAY·shun) *n.* the combining of a substance with oxygen. Common types of oxidation are burning and the formation of rust.

oxygen (OKS·ih·jen) *n.* a colorless, odorless, gaseous element that makes up one-fifth of the earth's atmosphere. Animals need oxygen to survive.

oxygen cycle (OKS·ih·jen SY·kul) *n.* the process in which plants give off oxygen that is taken in by animals, which then breathe out carbon dioxide, which, when used by plants, produces more oxygen.

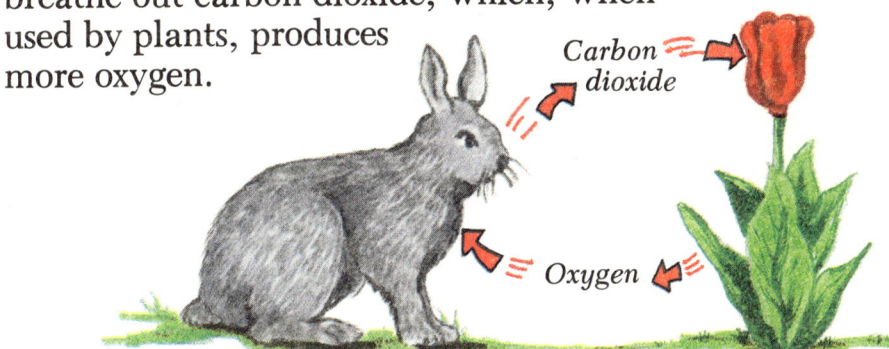

ozone (OH·zohn) *n.* a form of oxygen found in a thick layer in the upper atmosphere and in smaller amounts near the earth's surface. Ozone in the upper atmosphere prevents the sun's harmful ultraviolet rays from reaching the earth, but ozone near the ground is a dangerous pollutant.

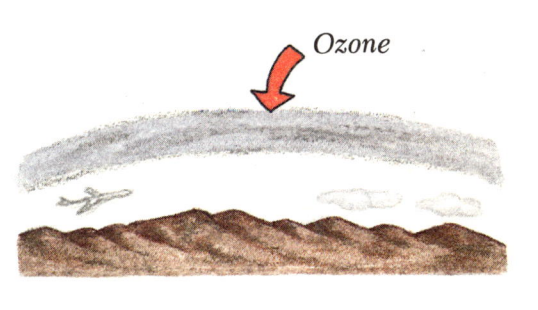

Pp

pack ice (PAK EYSS) *n.* a large mass of ice formed by the freezing of sea water.

paleontology (PAY•lee•un•TOL•uh•jee) *n.* the study of ancient life forms, as represented by their fossils.

parallax (PAYR•uh•laks) *n.* the apparent shift in position of a distant object because of a change in position of the observer. Early astronomers used the principle of parallax to measure the distance from the earth to the sun.

parallel (PAYR•uh•lel) *adj.* parallel lines are at an equal distance from each other at all points and never touch.

parallelogram (payr•uh•LEL•oh•gram) *n.* a four-sided figure in which each side is parallel and equal in length to the side opposite it.

parasite (PAYR•uh•syt) *n.* a living plant or animal that feeds on or in another living thing. Fleas are parasites, as is mistletoe, which takes water from the plant it lives on.

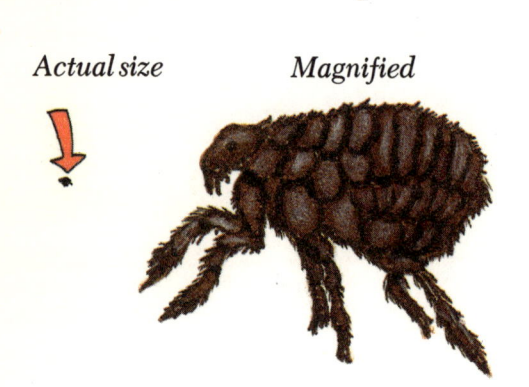

Actual size *Magnified*

Dog flea

Mistletoe attached to another plant

parsec (PAR•sek) *n.* a unit of measure used to describe great distances in space. A parsec is about 3.26 light-years.

Pasteur, Louis (pas•TEWR, LOO•ee) *1822–1895* French chemist who proved that bacteria can travel through the air, spoiling food. He showed that heat could destroy these creatures in food, especially milk. That process became known as pasteurization. He realized that bacteria also cause many contagious diseases.

payload (PAY·lohd) *n.* any cargo carried by a vehicle, particularly an airplane or spacecraft.

peninsula (peh·NIN·soo·luh) *n.* a narrow body of land that is surrounded by water on three sides.

perennial (puh·REN·ee·ul) *adj.* occurring regularly over a span of years. Perennial plants die back at the end of each growing season and then regrow again the following year because their roots survive the winter months.

period (PEER·ee·ud) *n.* a unit of time. The dinosaurs lived during the Mesozoic era, which is divided into three periods, each lasting millions of years.

Mesozoic era

*Cretaceous period—
45 million years ago*

*Jurassic period—
50 million years ago*

*Triassic period—
63 million years ago*

periodic table (peer·ee·AHD·ik TAY·bul) *n.* the arrangement of elements in order of their atomic number, which is the number of protons in the nucleus.

perpendicular (per·pen·DIK·yew·lar) *adj.* at right angles to each other. At each corner of a square or rectangle, the two sides that meet are perpendicular.

petroleum (peh•TROH•lee•um) *n.* an oily liquid that formed in the earth from living things that died millions of years ago. It is converted into many important fuels, such as gasoline and kerosene, and it is used in the manufacture of some plastics.

phosphor (FOS•for) *n.* a material that glows when exposed to ultraviolet light or other forms of energy. Phosphors can be seen in certain rocks.

photosynthesis (foh•toh•SIN•thuh•sis) *n.* the process by which green plants produce food from carbon dioxide, water, and sunlight. Oxygen is given off by the plant during photosynthesis.

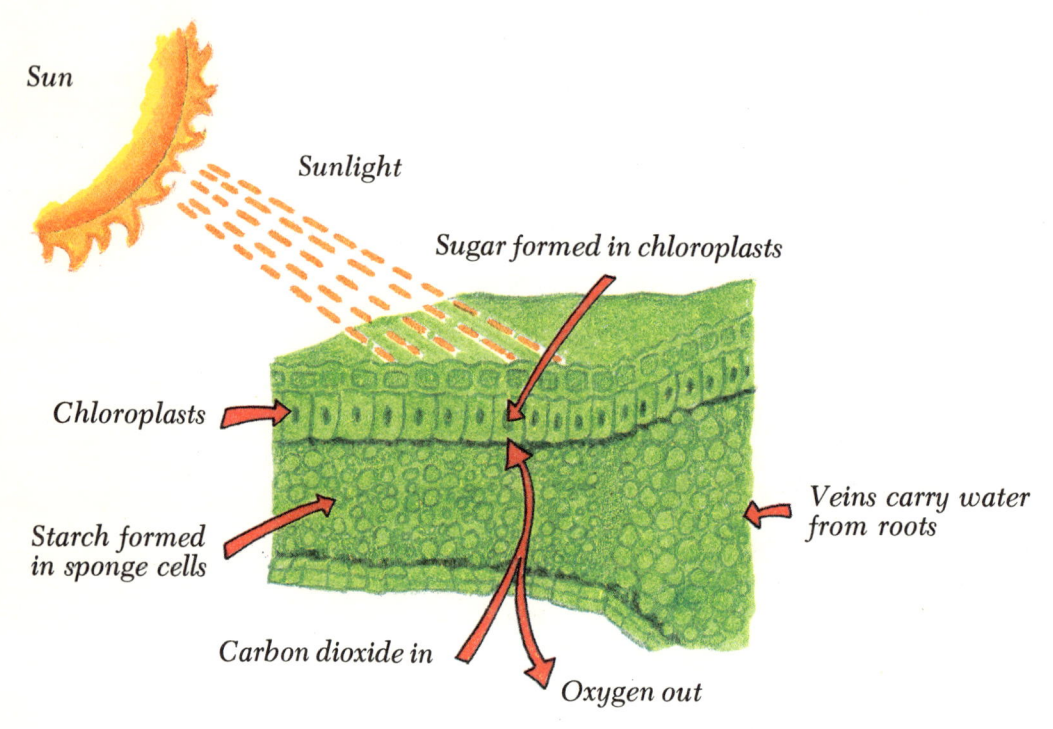

Sun
Sunlight
Sugar formed in chloroplasts
Chloroplasts
Veins carry water from roots
Starch formed in sponge cells
Carbon dioxide in
Oxygen out

Cross section of a leaf

phylum (FY•lum) *n.* a main division of the animal kingdom. Each phylum is made up of smaller groups called classes, which in turn are made up of even smaller groups called orders, which are made up of still smaller groups called families.

physical change (FIZ•ih•kul CHAYNJ) *n.* a change in a substance that does not cause a chemical change in its individual molecules. For example, melting a solid into a liquid or tearing a piece of paper is a physical change.

physics (FIZ•iks) *n.* the study of the natural laws that govern matter and energy.

physiology (FIZ•ee•OL•oh•jee) *n.* the study of how and why living things are able to function.

pistil (PIS•til) *n.* the center part of a flower that holds the ovules. The pistil is where seeds will form when the ovules have been fertilized. It forms the fruit of the plant.

Pistil
Stamens
Ovule
Cross section of a flower

pit (PIT) *n.* a deep hole or shaft in a mine.

n. the hard, covered seed in the center of certain fruits such as peaches and avocados.

Peach pit
Avocado pit

pitch (PICH) *n.* the highness or lowness of a sound. The length of the sound waves determine the pitch. Short waves are high and long waves are low.

planet (PLAA•net) *n.* a relatively large body in space that revolves around a star. Earth is a planet that revolves around the sun.

plankton (PLANK•tun) *n.* microscopic plants or animals that drift in large bodies of water such as oceans or lakes. Plankton are an important food for many other water animals.

plant (PLANT) *n.* a living thing that, with the exception of fungi, produces its own food by photosynthesis.

Cotton plant

plasma (PLAZ•muh) *n.* the fluid part of the blood that contains salts, sugars, proteins, and some waste products.

plate (PLAYT) *n.* a huge section of the earth's crust that floats on the mantle and moves very slowly. There are seven major plates on the earth.

American
Eurasian
Indian
Pacific
African
Antarctic
Nazca

Earth's seven major plates

n. a section of hard, protective covering in certain animals.

Armadillo covered with bony plates

plateau (plaa•TOH) *n.* a level, flat-topped highland area.

plumage (PLOO•mij) *n.* the feathers of a bird. Male birds often have more colorful plumage than females.

Male junglefowl

pneumatic (noo•MAT•ik) *adj.* operated by air, especially by the pressure of compression.

pole (POHL) *n.* one of the two points where the force field of a magnet is centered. One pole is positive, and one is negative.

pollen (POLL•un) *n.* powdery grains containing the male reproductive cells of seed-producing plants. Pollen is produced by a part of the flower called the stamen. Pollen grains land on the pistil and send sperm cells into the ovules.

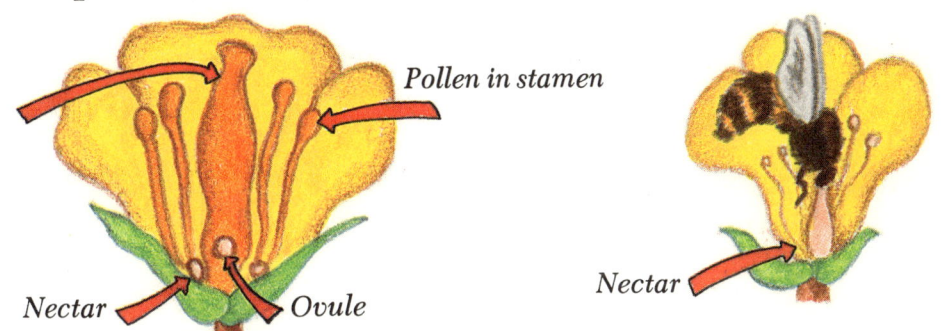

Pollen in stamen

Nectar *Ovule* *Nectar*

Cross section of a flower **Bee pollinates flower**

pollinate (POLL•uh•nayt) *v.* to transfer pollen from the stamen to the pistil of a flower so that seeds may develop. In searching for nectar, a bee brushes against pollen on the stamen and deposits it on the pistil.

pollution (poh•LOO•shun) *n.* additions to the environment that are harmful. Exhaust fumes from cars are an example of pollution.

pores (PORZ) *n.* tiny openings in the surface of something. Humans have millions of pores in the skin.

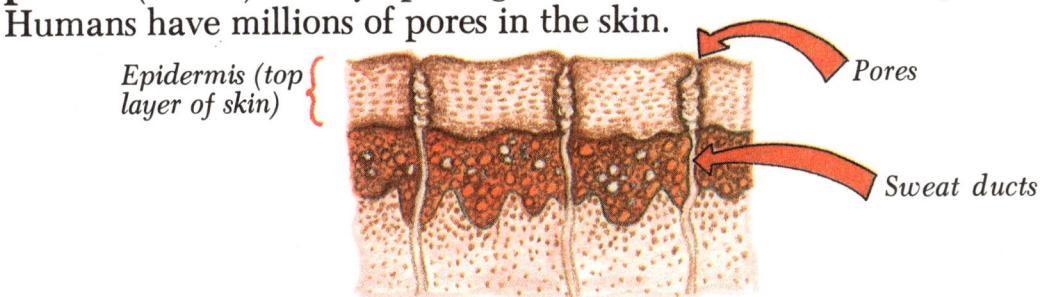

Epidermis (top layer of skin) *Pores*

Sweat ducts

Cross section of human skin

potential energy (poh•TEN•shul EN•er•jee) *n.* the energy an object contains by virtue of its location relative to other objects. A brick held in your hand has potential energy, which you can see if you drop it.

precipitation (prih•sip•uh•TAY•shun) *n.* any form that water vapor may take when condensing and falling to the earth. Rain, snow, and fog are all forms of precipitation.

predator (PRED•uh•tor) *n.* an animal that hunts and kills other animals for food. Lions are predators.

Lion

Cougar

Leopard

Animal predators

predict (prih•DIKT) *v.* to make a guess at what will happen in the future. By studying present weather conditions, meteorologists can often predict upcoming storms.

pressure (PRESH•er) *n.* the amount of steady force applied to an area. One unit used to measure pressure is pounds per square inch.

prey (PRAY) *n.* an animal that is hunted and eaten by another animal. Zebras are a common prey of lions.

primary colors (PRY•mayr•ee KUL•erz) *n. science:* the red, green, and blue colors of light that when mixed together produce white light.

n. art: the red, blue, and yellow colors of paint that when mixed together produce the color black.

prism (PRIZ•um) *n.* a solid, pyramidal-shaped transparent object. When made of glass a prism is able to bend light rays and break white light into the different colors of the spectrum.

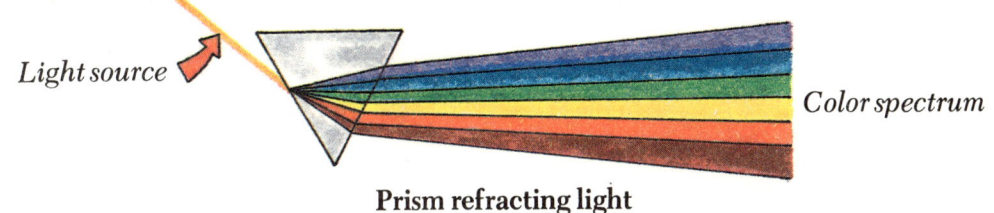

Light source

Color spectrum

Prism refracting light

probe (PROHB) *n.* a device or instrument used for exploration. For example, dentists use probes to examine any cavities that they find.

n. a space vehicle that is used to collect data about our solar system.

property (PROP•er•tee) *n.* the characteristic of a material that is used to identify it, such as its density or boiling point.

proteins (PROH•teenz) *n.* large chains of amino acids. Amino acids are simple compounds that are the building blocks of life. All amino acids contain the elements carbon, nitrogen, oxygen, and hydrogen.

proton (PROH•tahn) *n.* an elementary particle with a positive charge found in the nucleus of an atom.

protoplasm (proh•toh•PLAZ•um) *n.* the jellylike material that makes up the cells of all living things. Protoplasm includes the cell membrane that surrounds and protects the cell, the nucleus that contains the genetic information necessary for life, and the fluid inside the cell, called cytoplasm.

pulley (PULL•ee) *n.* a simple machine made up of a grooved wheel and a rope or chain. A pulley is used to change the direction of a force. Using a pulley makes it easier to lift a heavy weight.

Grooved wheel

A simple pulley machine

pupa (PEW•puh) *n.* a stage in the metamorphosis of certain insects between larva and adult. During this period, the creature lives inside a hard protective case, does not eat, and changes its physical form completely. For example, caterpillars are larval insects that live in a cocoon during the pupa stage, and later emerge in their adult form as butterflies.

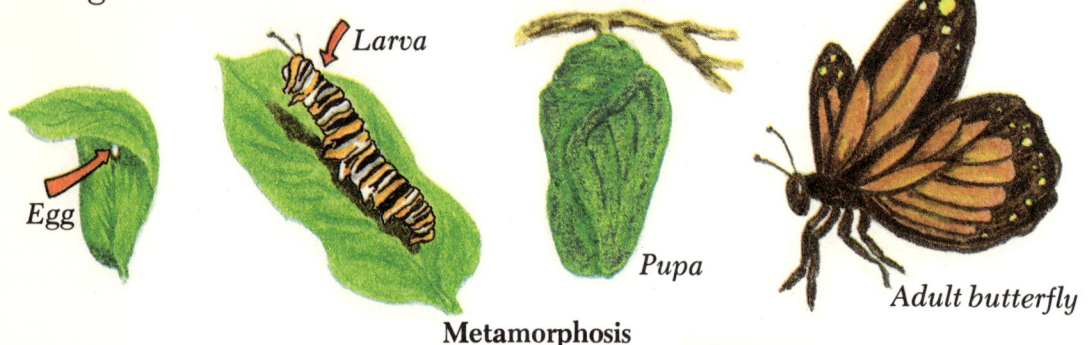

Egg

Larva

Pupa

Adult butterfly

Metamorphosis

pupil (PEW•pul) *n.* the opening in the center of the eye through which light passes.

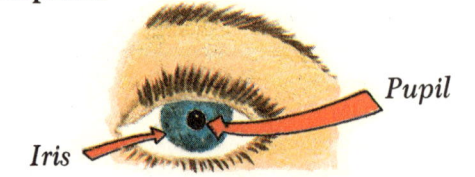

Iris

Pupil

pyramid (PEER•uh•mid) *n.* a solid shape made from a base and at least three triangular-shaped sides that meet in a point at the top. The base can be many different shapes, including a triangle, square, or rectangle.

Qq

quadrant (KWAD•rant) *n.* one section of an area that has been divided into four parts.

quantity (KWAN•tih•tee) *n.* the amount of a material, substance, or object.

quarry (KWOR•ee) *n.* a place where rocks or ores are mined.

n. the prey that an animal is hunting.

quartz (KWORTZ) *n.* a hard, translucent mineral containing silicon.

Smoky quartz

quasar (KWAY•zar) *n.* galaxylike, distant object in space that is very bright, gives off tremendous amounts of energy, and travels at incredible speeds.

Rr

radar (RAY•dar) *n.* **ra**dio **d**etecting **a**nd **r**anging. A system for locating moving objects such as boats, airplanes, and satellites. Radar works by sending out radio waves, which bounce off the object, and then measuring the time of the waves' return from the object and the direction from which they come.

radioactivity (ray•dee•oh•ak•TIV•ih•tee) *n.* the breakdown of the nucleus of certain elements, causing the release of tiny particles of mass and/or electromagnetic radiation. Certain types of radioactive materials are harmful to living organisms.

radio waves (RAY•dee•oh WAYVZ) *n.* a type of energy that travels in waves through air or space and can carry radio and television signals.

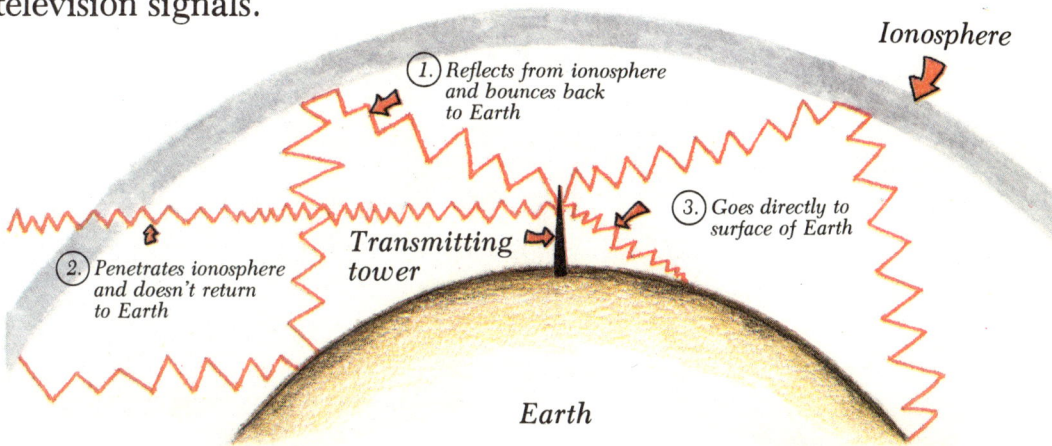

Ionosphere

1. Reflects from ionosphere and bounces back to Earth
2. Penetrates ionosphere and doesn't return to Earth
3. Goes directly to surface of Earth

Transmitting tower

Earth

Three types of radio waves

rain (RAYN) *n.* drops of water that form when water vapor in the upper atmosphere condenses and then falls to earth.

rainbow (RAYN·boh) *n.* an arched color effect in the sky formed when light rays from the sun shine on raindrops and are broken down into the colors of the spectrum.

rain forest (RAYN FOR·est) *n.* forest found in tropical regions near the equator, which has plenty of water and rich, thick vegetation. Rain forests are divided into at least three different levels according to the type of vegetation. Different sorts of animals live in each level.

In the treetops — *Squirrel monkey*

Under the canopy — *Tamandua*

On the forest floor — *Goliath beetle*, *Giant snail*

Animals of the rain forest

rare gases (RAYR GAS·ez) *n.* also called noble or inert gases, they are elements that occur in small amounts in the atmosphere. They are: helium, neon, argon, krypton, xenon, and radon. Together, rare gases make up less than one percent of the atmosphere.

ratio (RAY·shee·oh) *n.* the numerical comparison of two quantities, one divided by the other. If people at a picnic eat two hamburgers for each hot dog eaten, the ratio of hamburgers to hot dogs eaten is two to one.

reaction (ree•AK•shun) *n.* an opposite response to a force.

n. a result that occurs when two or more substances are combined and chemically changed. When bicarbonate and vinegar are combined, the reaction is the release of carbon dioxide gas.

rectangle (REK•tayn•gul) *n.* a four-sided figure with a right angle at each corner. The opposite sides are of equal length.

recycle (ree•SY•kul) *v.* to use a material more than once.

red giant (RED JY•ant) *n.* a very large, older star that has used up most of the hydrogen fuel at its core.

reef (REEF) *n.* a buildup of rock or coral. Coral reefs usually form around islands in clear, warm salt water.

reentry (ree•EN•tree) *n.* the return of a space vehicle into the earth's atmosphere.

reflect (rih•FLEKT) *v.* to bounce back from a surface. The moon appears to shine because it reflects light rays from the sun.

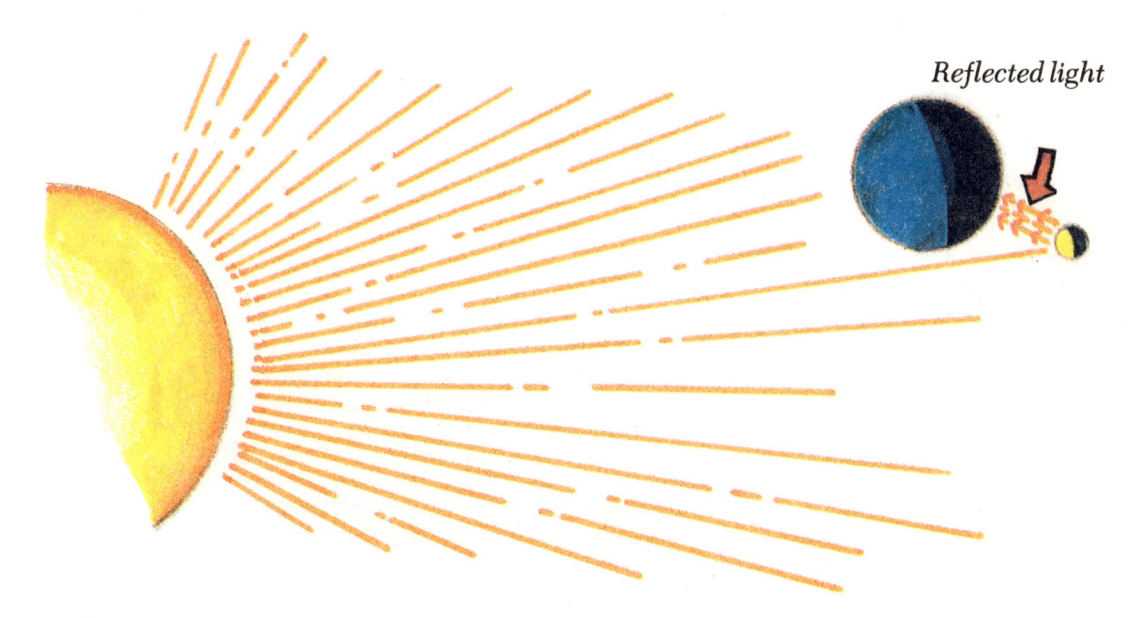

Reflected light

reflex (REE•fleks) *n.* an automatic reaction by an organism in response to a specific signal or stimulus. Reflex action causes you to pull your hand away when you touch something too hot.

refraction (ree•FRAK•shun) *n.* the bending of light when it passes from one material through another material of different density. Due to the difference in density between air and water, a spoon in a glass of water appears to be bent at the surface of the water.

repel (ruh•PEL) *v.* to force or push something away. In magnets, like poles repel each other.

reproduce (ree•proh•DOOSS) *v.* to duplicate; to make more of something. Bacteria reproduce by dividing.

reptile (REP•tyl) *n.* a cold-blooded, egg-laying animal that breathes air, has a backbone, and is usually covered by a layer of scales or plates.

Collared lizard

Eastern box turtle

Flap-necked chameleon

Indian cobra snake

Reptiles

research (REE•serch) *v.* to investigate something or search for the answer to a problem. To look for information that has already been recorded. Researching is done in a library or a laboratory.

reservoir (REZ•erv•war) *n.* a place where fluid is stored. A city's drinking water is often stored in a large lake reservoir. The fuel reservoir in a car is the gas tank.

resin (REZ•in) *n.* a sticky material, usually a form of sap, produced by plants. Certain types of resin are used to make varnish.

resistance (ree•ZIS•tanss) *n.* something that prevents or slows the flow of energy or the motion of an object.

resources (REE•sorss•ez) *n.* useful parts of an environment such as an abundant supply of fresh water, vegetation, or mineral deposits.

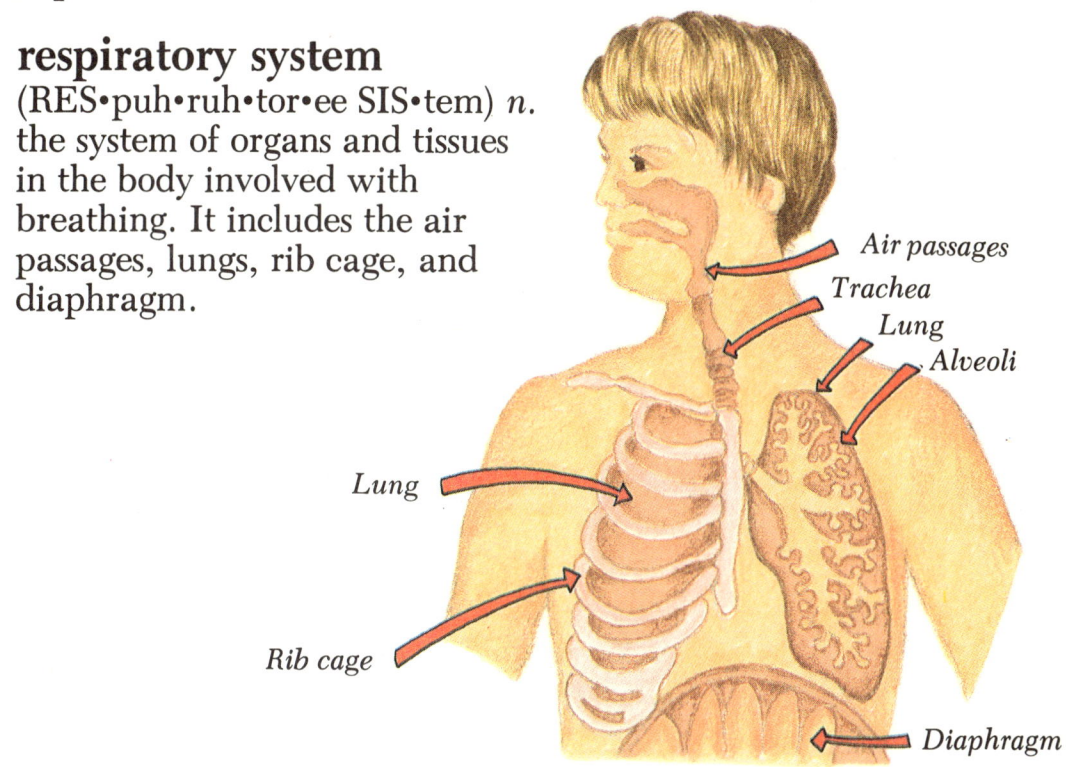

respiratory system (RES•puh•ruh•tor•ee SIS•tem) *n.* the system of organs and tissues in the body involved with breathing. It includes the air passages, lungs, rib cage, and diaphragm.

The human respiratory system

response (rih•SPONSS) *n.* the answer or reaction to a stimulus or signal.

retina (RET•ih•nuh) *n.* a layer of light-sensitive nerve and supporting cells at the back of the inside of the eye. The retina captures the image that is sent by light, and the optic nerve sends it to the brain.

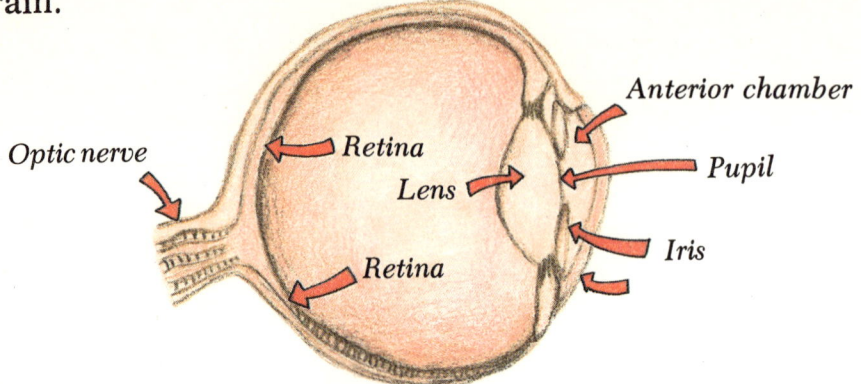

The human eye

retrograde motion (REH•troh•grayd MOH•shun) *n.* movement opposite to the standard eastward movement, or *direct motion*, of the earth and other bodies of the solar system. Also, the temporary, apparent movement of a body in a direction opposite to usual.

revolution (rev•oh•LOO•shun) *n.* one complete trip of an object in space around another object in space. Earth takes about 365 days to make one revolution around the sun.

Richter scale (RIK•ter SKAYL) *n.* a scale from one to ten used to describe the strength of an earthquake. Earthquakes measuring less than five on the Richter scale often produce only minor damage.

robot (ROH•bot) *n.* a machine designed to do certain chores automatically.

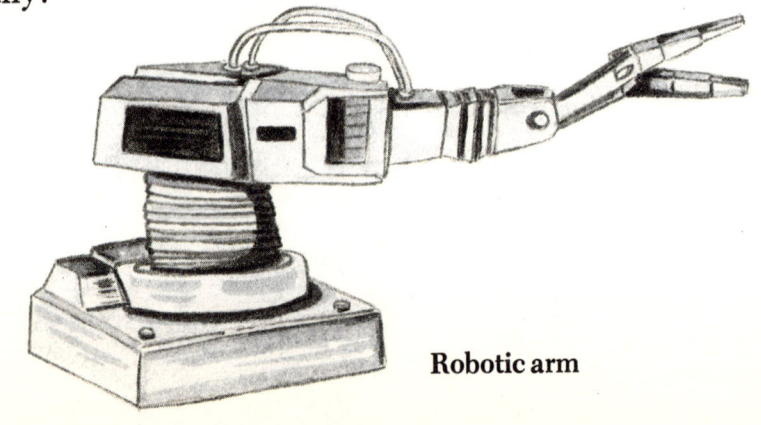

Robotic arm

rock (ROK) *n.* an accumulation of minerals formed by heat and/or pressure.

rods (RODZ) *n.* nerve endings in the retina of the eye that detect dim light and allow one to see at night. Rods do not distinguish color.

root (ROOT) *n.* the part of a plant that grows in the soil, takes in water and minerals, and anchors the plant to the ground.

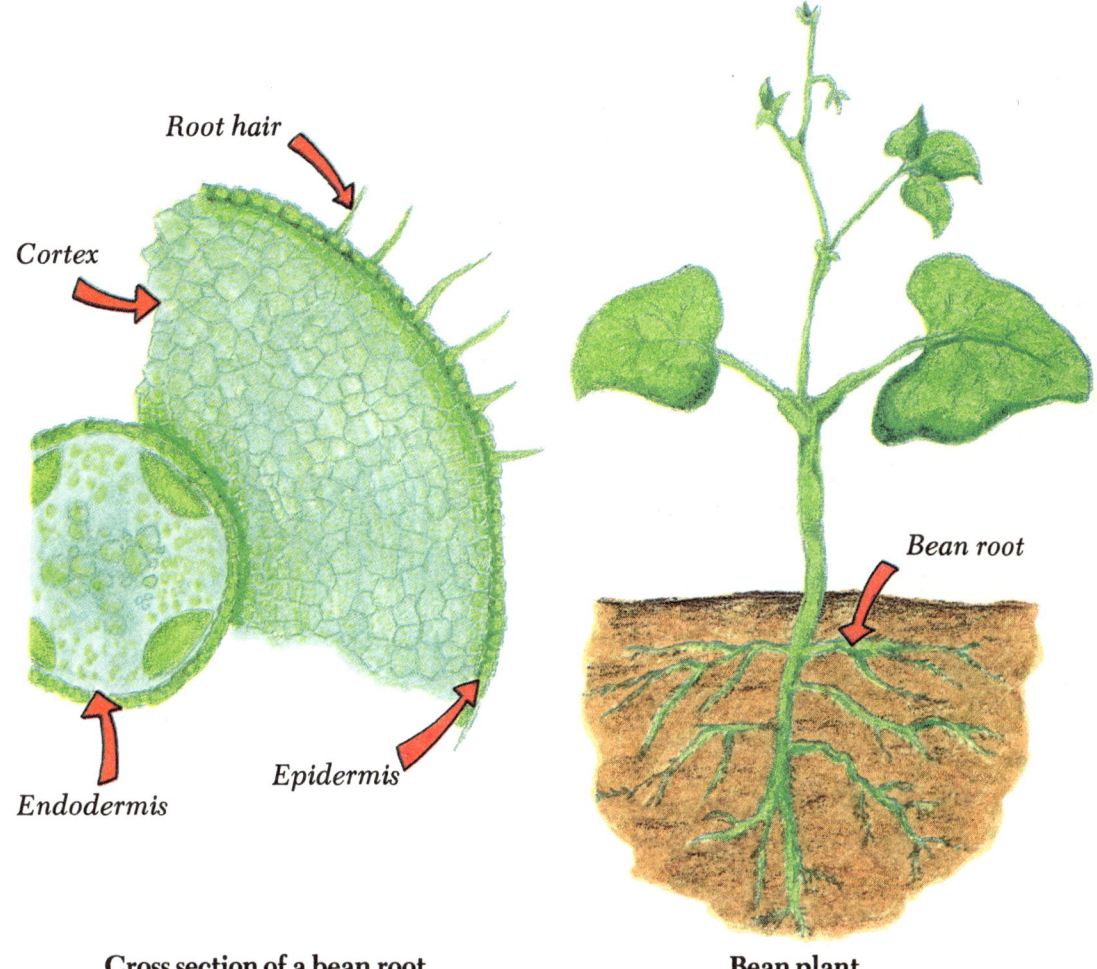

Root hair

Cortex

Endodermis

Epidermis

Bean root

Cross section of a bean root   **Bean plant**

root hairs (ROOT HAYRZ) *n.* tiny hairlike fibers on the roots of a plant that absorb water from the soil.

rotate (ROH•tayt) *v.* to revolve or spin. The earth rotates around an imaginary line, its axis, once every twenty-four hours.

rust (RUST) *n.* a reddish-brown substance produced by the reaction of iron with oxygen in the air. Another name for rust is iron oxide.

Rutherford, Ernest (RUH•thur•furd, ER•nest) *1871-1937* English physicist who discovered that some atoms are unstable (that is, radioactive) but slowly become stable over time. He found that one could determine how old a substance is by measuring the rate at which it releases radioactive particles. In his model of the atom, a center (nucleus) is surrounded by orbiting electrons.

Ss

saliva (suh•LY•vuh) *n.* a liquid produced by glands in the mouth that contains enzymes to begin the process of digestion, and that helps soften food and make it easier to swallow.

sap (SAP) *n.* the fluid in a plant that carries food and water throughout the plant.

satellite (SAT•uh•lyt) *n.* a body in space that revolves around another object. The moon is Earth's natural satellite. Satellites may also be artificial objects such as communications satellites.

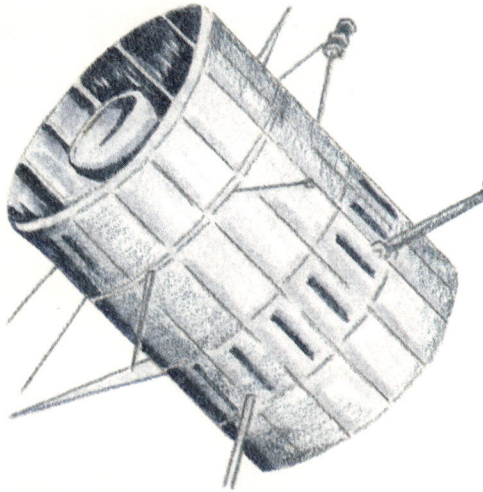

Explorer—the first successful American satellite (1958)

scarp (SKARP) *n.* a slope or ridge that cuts across and exposes layers of sedimentary rock by faulting or erosion.

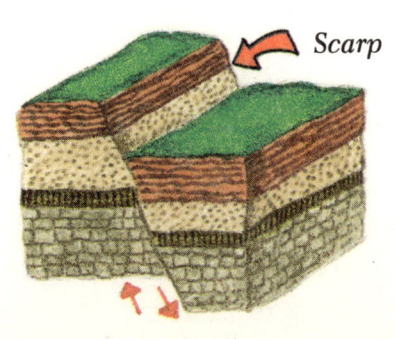

Scarp

Fault

scavenger (SKAV•un•jer) *n.* an animal that feeds on the remains of dead animals or on waste material. A vulture is a scavenger.

school (SKOOL) *n.* a large group of fish swimming together.

sea level (SEE LEV•ul) *n.* the average surface level of the water of the earth's oceans.

seamount (SEE•mownt) *n.* an underwater mountain.

season (SEE•zun) *n.* one of four annual climatic periods, Spring, Summer, Fall, and Winter, which are caused by the position of the earth in relation to the sun.

n. a period of time that is known for a particular type of weather or activity, such as the dry season, hurricane season, or growing season.

secrete (see•KREET) *v.* to produce and release a substance from certain cells of plants or animals. In mammals, the liver secretes bile into the intestines, which helps to digest fat.

sedimentary (SED•ih•MEN•ter•ee) *adj.* describes a kind of rock formed when layers of individual particles are pressed together into hard, solid layers. Limestone is a sedimentary rock.

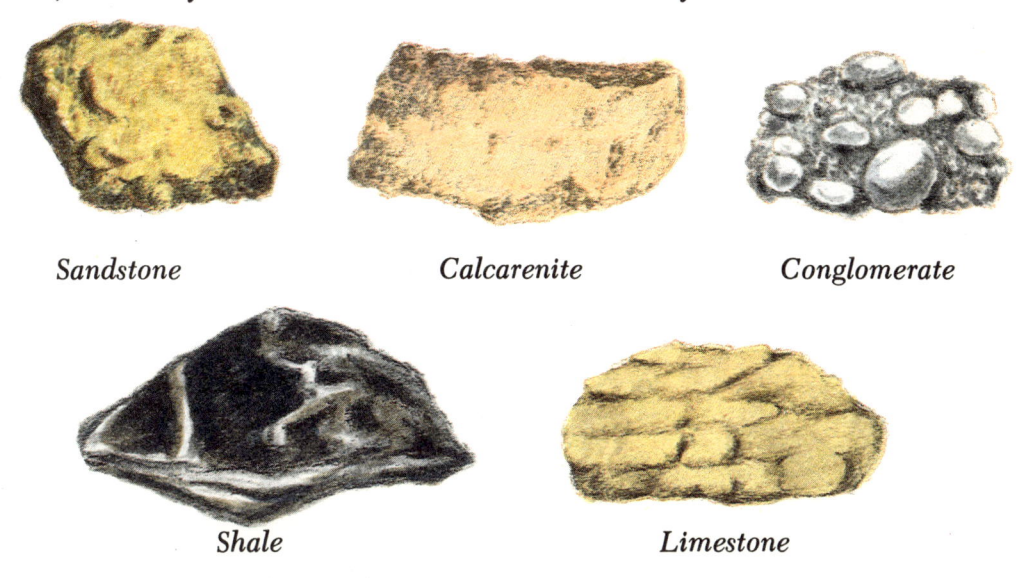

Sandstone *Calcarenite* *Conglomerate*

Shale *Limestone*

Some types of sedimentary rock

91

seed (SEED) *n.* the fertilized reproductive cell of a plant that can grow into a new plant.

1. Seed is planted
2. Seed absorbs water, swells, and roots appear
3. Roots continue to grow, stem appears above ground
4. Stem grows higher, leaves appear

The germination of a seed

seed coat (SEED COHT) *n.* the protective outer covering of a seed.

senses (SEN•sez) *n.* the information-gathering systems of the body that make it aware of its surroundings. The five senses are touch, taste, smell, hearing, and sight.

sensor (SEN•ser) *n.* a device used to locate or identify objects or forms of energy. Some rockets have heat sensors, which track infrared energy.

Heat sensor

sepal (SEE•pul) *n.* the part of a flowering plant that protects the flower buds.

Sepal

set (SET) *n.* a collection of objects or numbers.

sextant (SEK•stant) *n.* an instrument used especially in navigation to find position by measuring the angular distance of the sun or certain stars in relation to the horizon.

shadow (SHAH•doh) *n.* a dark area formed when light rays are blocked by an object.

Light source   *Shadow*

short circuit (SHORT SER•kit) *n.* an alternate or shorter and usually unintentional path in an electric circuit that has lower electrical resistance and diverts current away from the rest of the circuit.

simple machine (SIM•pul muh•SHEEN) *n.* a device used to change the direction of a force or to increase force or distance. A lever and a screw are simple machines. A hammer is one type of lever.

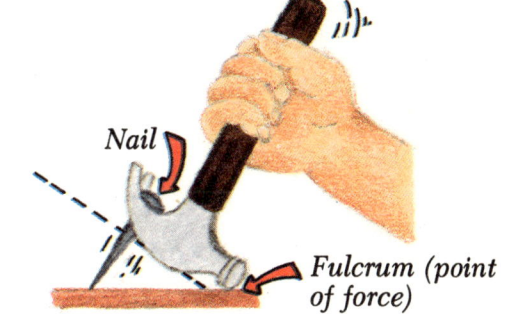

Nail   *Fulcrum (point of force)*

Claw hammer

skeleton (SKEL•uh•tun) *n.* the framework of bones that supports the body and gives it its shape.

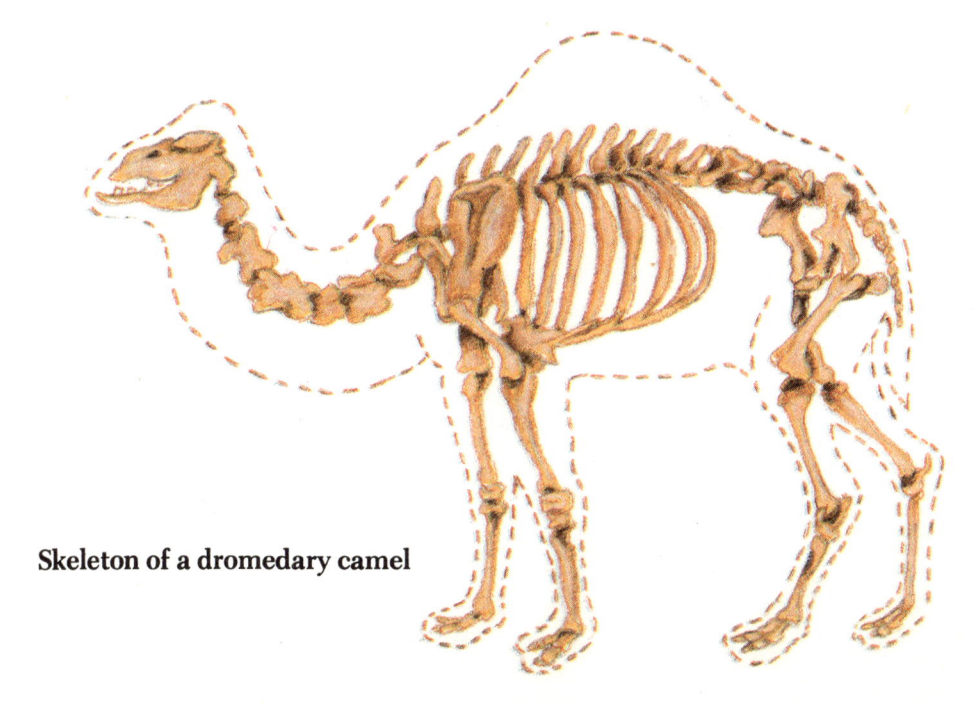

Skeleton of a dromedary camel

sleep (SLEEP) *n.* a period of decreased awareness during which the body rests.

sleet (SLEET) *n.* bits of ice that form from rain freezing before it hits the earth.

smog (SMOG) *n.* a form of pollution in which smoke, harmful particles, and gases combine with fog.

snow (SNOH) *n.* six-sided ice crystals that form from water vapor in the air. When they are heavy enough and the temperature is cold enough, the crystals fall to earth as snowflakes.

Snowflake

soil (SOYL) *n.* loose material on the earth's surface formed from tiny particles of rocks and minerals, and the remains of living things.

solar energy (SOH•lar EN•er•jee) *n.* energy from the sun.

solar system (SOH•lar SIS•tem) *n.* the sun and all of the objects in orbit around it.

Our solar system

solar wind (SOH•lar WIND) *n.* a steady stream of charged particles that flows from the sun out into the solar system.

solid (SOL•id) *n.* a form of matter in which a material has a definite shape and volume.

solute (SOL•yewt) *n.* a substance that is dissolved in a liquid. Sugar is a common solute in many soft drinks.

solvent (SOL•vent) *n.* a substance, usually a liquid, that has the power to dissolve certain other substances within it. Water is a solvent.

sonar (SOH•nar) *n.* a system for locating things (or measuring distance) underwater by bouncing sound waves off of an object and calculating how long it takes before the echo returns.

sound (SOWND) *n.* a form of energy that travels in waves of vibration. Because molecules of matter must be available to pass the vibration along, there is no sound in a vacuum. The ear is an organ that detects sound vibrations and sends the signals to the brain.

n. a channel of water that connects two larger bodies of water or separates an island from the mainland.

Long Island Sound

Southeastern New York

Long Island

Atlantic Ocean

Channel

space (SPAYSS) *n.* everything beyond the earth's atmosphere.

95

spacecraft (SPAYSS·kraft) *n.* any object designed to travel through space.

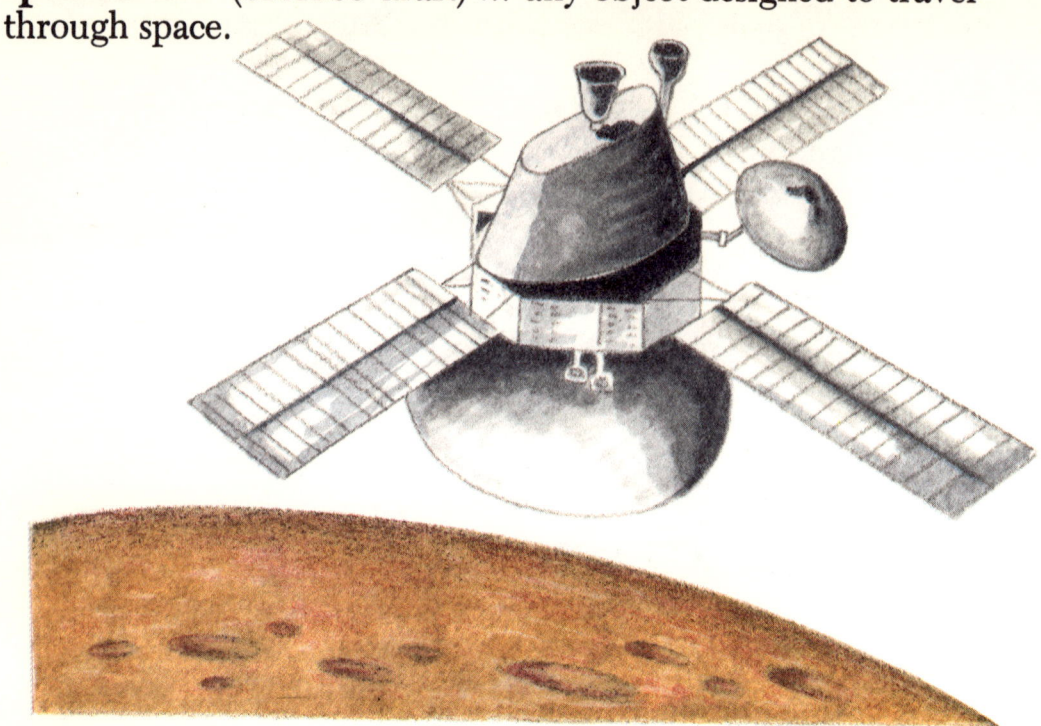

Spacecraft Mariner above planet Mercury

spawn (SPAHN) *v.* to lay eggs in water, as fish, mollusks, and amphibians do.

spectrum (SPEK·trum) *n.* the collection of all the different types of radiation that travel in waves, arranged in order of increasing wavelength. The longest waves are radio waves, and the shortest are gamma rays. Many waves are invisible, but some light waves can be seen as color. These make up the *visible* spectrum. In the visible spectrum the longest waves are red and the shortest are violet. Angstroms (Å) are used to measure wavelength. One angstrom equals one ten-billionth ($\frac{1}{10,000,000,000}$) of a meter.

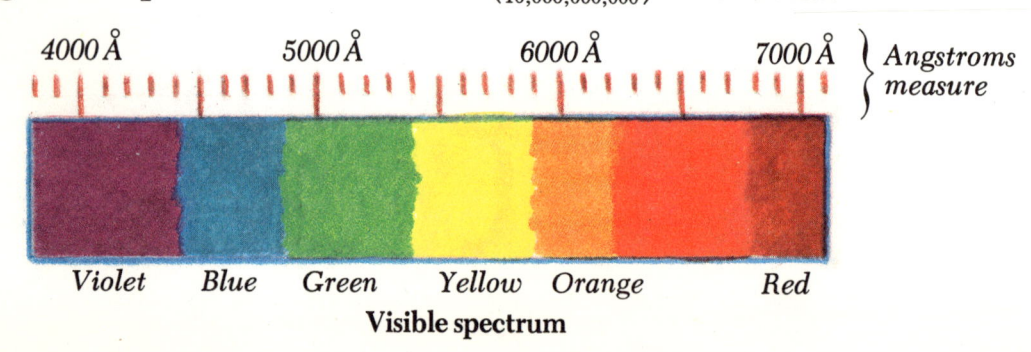

4000 Å   5000 Å   6000 Å   7000 Å   } *Angstroms measure*

Violet   Blue   Green   Yellow   Orange   Red
Visible spectrum

sperm (SPERM) *n.* a male reproductive cell.

96

sphere (SFEER) *n.* a solid, round object in which all points on the surface are an equal distance from the center.

spinal cord (SPY•nal KORD) *n.* a cord about one-half inch thick made up of nerve fibers that connect the brain to the rest of the body. The spinal cord is protected inside the backbone or spinal column.

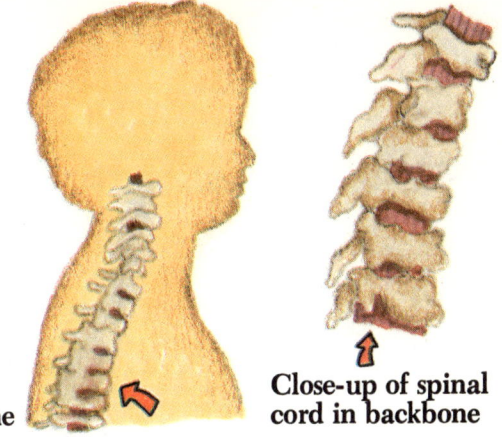

Spinal cord inside backbone

Close-up of spinal cord in backbone

spore (SPOR) *n.* the reproductive cell of certain plants such as ferns and mushrooms.

spring tide (SPRING TYD) *n.* very high tides that occur twice a month, during which time the sun, moon, and earth are in line with one other.

Sun
Moon
Earth
Spring tide

square (SKWAYR) *n.* a four-sided figure in which all sides are the same length and all angles are right angles.

stalactite (stuh•LAK•tyt) *n.* a stone formation that hangs from the roof of a limestone cave. Stalactites form when water containing calcite drips through the roof of the cave, forming iciclelike structures.

stalagmite (stuh•LAG•myt) *n.* a formation on a limestone cave floor. Stalagmites are formed when water containing calcite drips steadily to the floor in one spot.

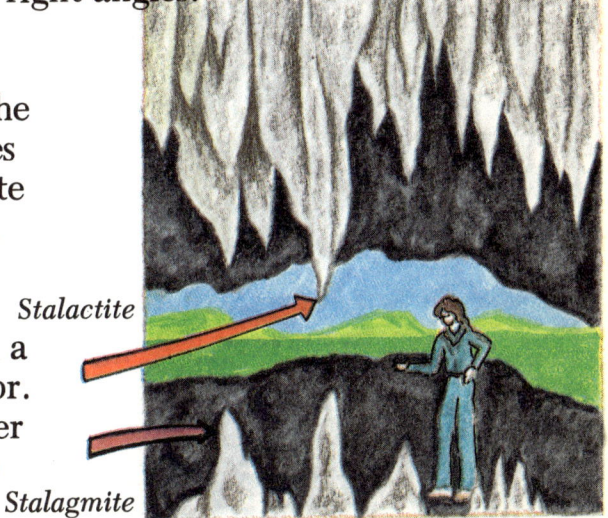

Stalactite

Stalagmite

Limestone cave

stamen (STAY•men) *n.* a flower's reproductive organ. Stamens produce pollen.

Stamen *Pistil*

star (STAR) *n.* a luminous body in space that is made up of very hot gases and gives off energy.

stem (STEM) *n.* the part of a plant that carries minerals and water from the roots, and food from the leaves, to the rest of the plant. Usually it supports the leaves or flowers and grows in the opposite direction of the root.

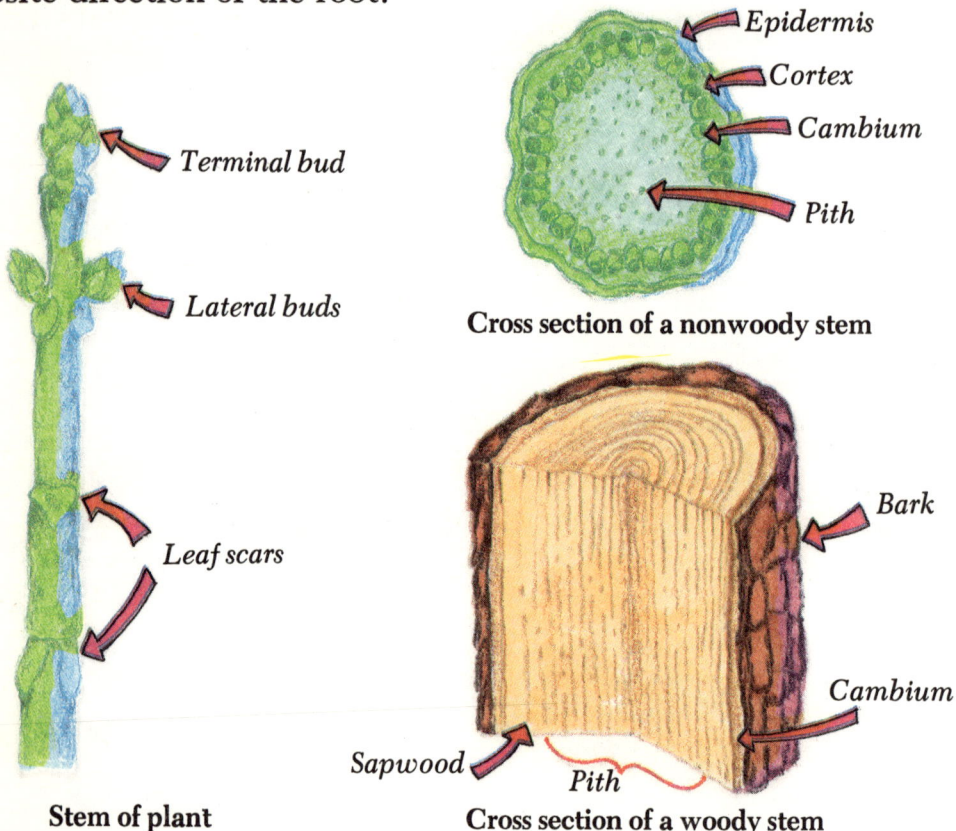

Terminal bud

Lateral buds

Leaf scars

Stem of plant

Epidermis
Cortex
Cambium
Pith

Cross section of a nonwoody stem

Bark
Cambium
Sapwood
Pith

Cross section of a woody stem

stethoscope (STETH•uh•skohp) *n.* a medical instrument used to listen to the heart and lungs.

stimulus (STIM•yew•lus) *n.* something that affects a living thing and produces a reaction. Any change in environment that produces a response.

strait (STRAYT) *n.* a narrow channel that connects two larger bodies of water. The Bering Strait between Alaska and Russia connects the Arctic Ocean with the Pacific Ocean.

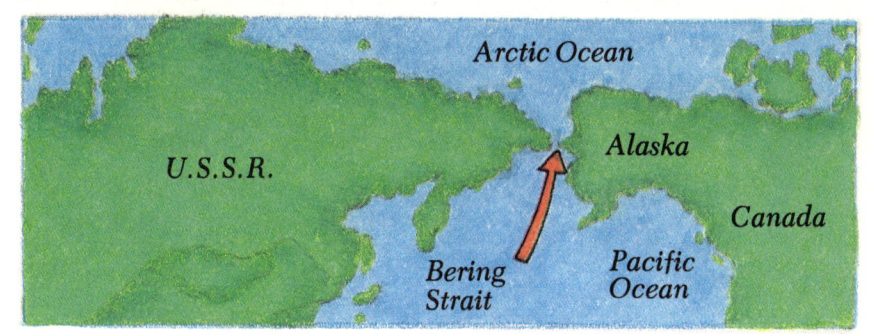

strata (STRAH•tuh) *n.* layers of sedimentary rock.

stratus (STRAH•tus) *n.* low-lying clouds that may appear to spread across the entire sky.

stress (STRESS) *n.* force acting on an area of an object that may cause it to wear, give way, or change shape.

structure (STRUK•cher) *n.* the way something is put together or joined.

subsoil (SUB•soyl) *n.* the layer of soil below the topsoil that contains no humus and is not good for growing plants.

Cross section of soil

Sun (SUN) *n.* the star around which Earth and all of the other planets in our solar system revolve and which supplies Earth with heat and light.

sunspot (SUN•spot) *n.* a patch on the surface of the sun that is darker and slightly cooler than the surrounding area.

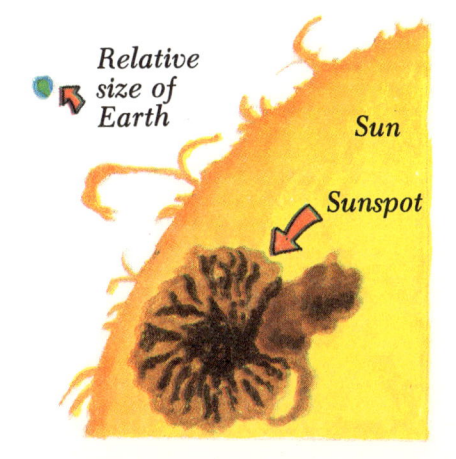

supernova (SOO•per•NOH•vuh) *n.* a huge explosion caused by the collapse of a massive star.

surface (SER•fuss) *n.* the top or outer layer of something.

symbiosis (sim•by•OH•sis) *n.* a relationship in which two living things live together and each one benefits the other. The alga and fungus that form lichen have a symbiotic relationship because the alga feeds the fungus, and the fungus keeps the alga moist.

synapse (SIH•naps) *n.* the space between nerves across which signals pass from one nerve to the next.

Tt

tadpole (TAD•pohl) *n.* an early stage in the life cycle of a frog or salamander. Tadpoles live in the water and have a tail and gills, which they later lose.

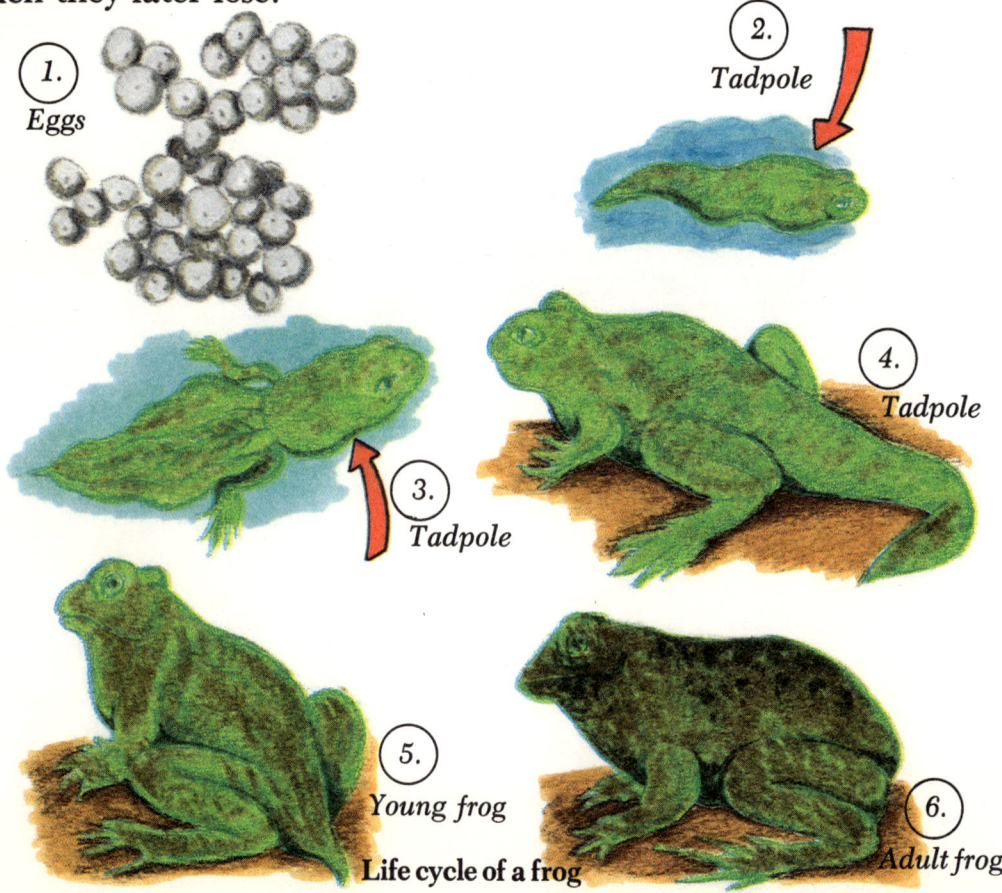

1. Eggs
2. Tadpole
3. Tadpole
4. Tadpole
5. Young frog
6. Adult frog

Life cycle of a frog

100

taste buds (TAYST BUDZ) *n.* tiny bumps on the surface of the tongue that are sensitive to sour, sweet, bitter, and salty tastes.

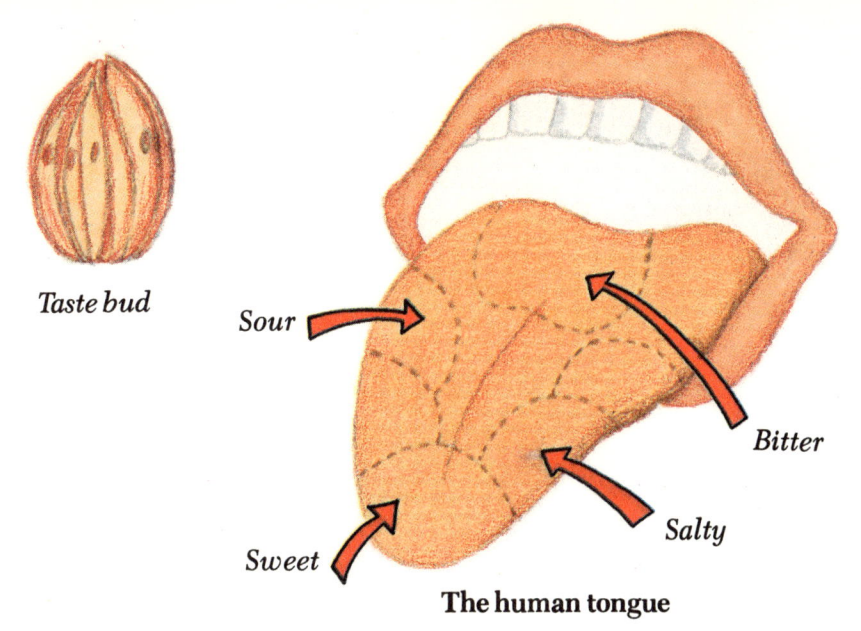

Taste bud

Sour *Bitter* *Salty* *Sweet*

The human tongue

tectonic (tek•TAHN•ik) *adj.* dealing with the movement of the very large sheets of solid and molten rock that make up the earth's crust.

telescope (TEL•uh•skohp) *n.* an instrument made up of lenses and mirrors that magnify distant objects.

temperature (TEM•per•cher) *n.* a measure of how fast the molecules in a substance are vibrating. The faster the movement, the warmer the temperature.

tendon (TEN•dun) *n.* a tough band of tissue that attaches skeletal muscles to bones.

terrestrial (tuh•RES•tree•ul) *adj.* having to do with Earth. Also having to do with land, as distinct from water or air.

theory (THEE•or•ee) *n.* an explanation of why or how something works.

thermocline (THER•moh•klyn) *n.* a layer in the ocean, from 300 to 650 feet below the surface, in which the temperature falls quickly as the depth increases.

thermometer (ther•MOM•et•er) *n.* an instrument used to measure temperature.

thunder (THUN•der) *n.* the rolling or cracking sound made when air expands quickly after being heated by a flash of lightning.

tides (TYDZ) *n.* the regular rise and fall of the earth's seas, caused by the rotation of the planet and the gravitational pull of the sun and the moon.

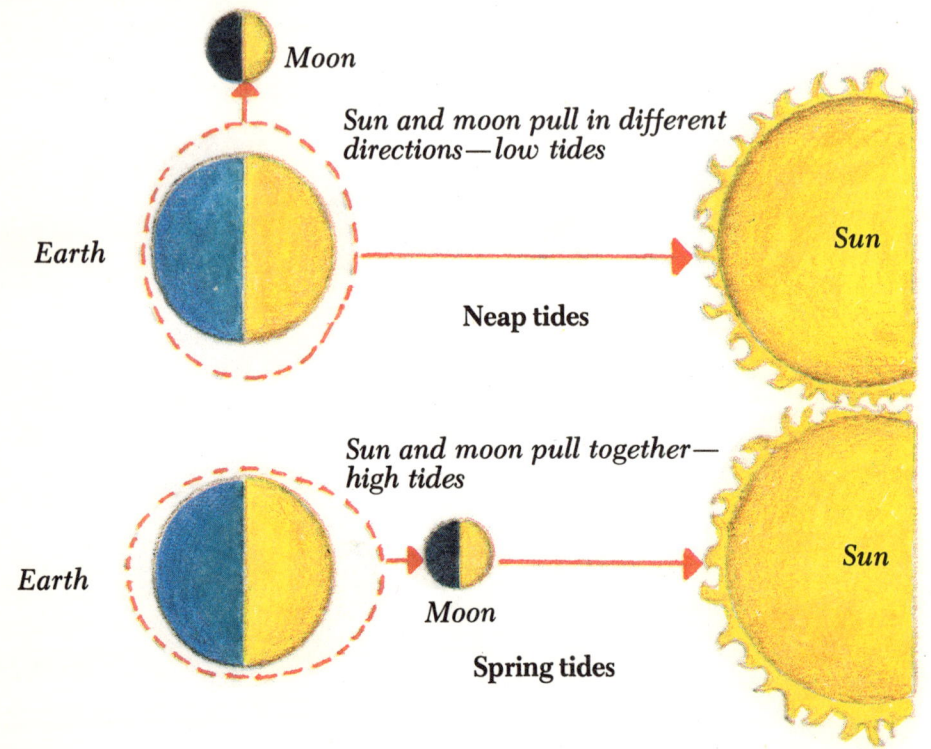

Moon

Sun and moon pull in different directions—low tides

Earth

Sun

Neap tides

Sun and moon pull together—high tides

Earth

Moon

Sun

Spring tides

tissue (TISH•yew) *n.* a group of similar cells in animals and plants that together form a definite type of structural material, such as skin tissue or muscle tissue.

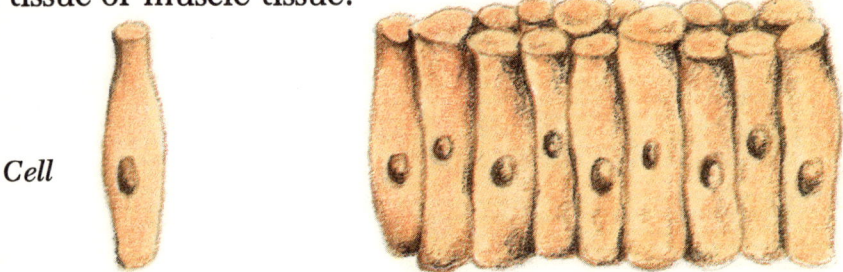

Cell

Tissue lining the esophagus

topsoil (TOP•soyl) *n.* the upper layer of soil that contains minerals and humus, and is good for growing plants.

tornado (tor•NAY•doh) *n.* a funnel-shaped windstorm. Along its path a tornado can cause damage due to high-speed winds and because of the fast, sharp drop in air pressure it produces.

toxic (TOK•sik) *adj.* poisonous, harmful.

trade winds (TRAYD WINDZ) *n.* belts of mild, steady winds that blow from the northeast above the equator and from the southeast below it.

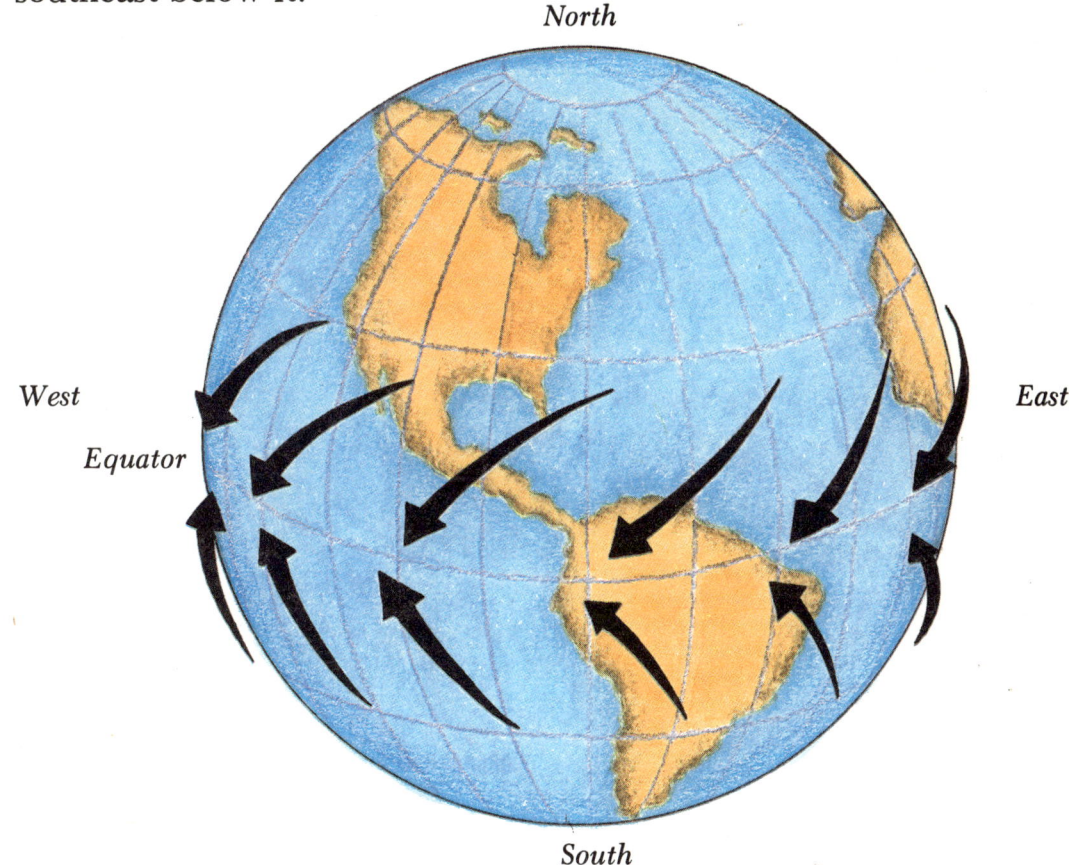

trajectory (truh•JEK•tuh•ree) *n.* the path of something that has been thrown or launched.

transistor (tran•ZIS•ter) *n.* a small valve through which the flow of electrical current can be controlled and the strength of an electrical signal can be increased.

103

translucent (tranz•LOOS•ent) *adj.* used to describe a material (such as tissue paper) that lets some light through but not enough for objects on the other side to be seen clearly.

transmitter (TRANZ•mitt•er) *n.* a device that sends electrical, radio, or television signals.

n. a living thing that transmits a disease to other living things. The tsetse fly is a transmitter of sleeping sickness.

transparent (tranz•PAYR•ent) *adj.* used to describe a material through which light passes easily and objects can be seen clearly. Glass is transparent.

tremor (TREM•er) *n.* a slight shaking or trembling movement.

trench (TRENCH) *n.* a deep, narrow valley in the ocean floor, formed where two of the earth's crustal plates meet and one rides over the other.

n. a long gouge in the earth's surface made by either humans or nature.

triangle (TRY•an•gul) *n.* a three-sided figure. The three interior angles add up to 180 degrees.

triceps (TRY•seps) *n.* a skeletal muscle in the back part of the arm above the elbow that causes the arm to straighten. The triceps reacts in opposition to the biceps.

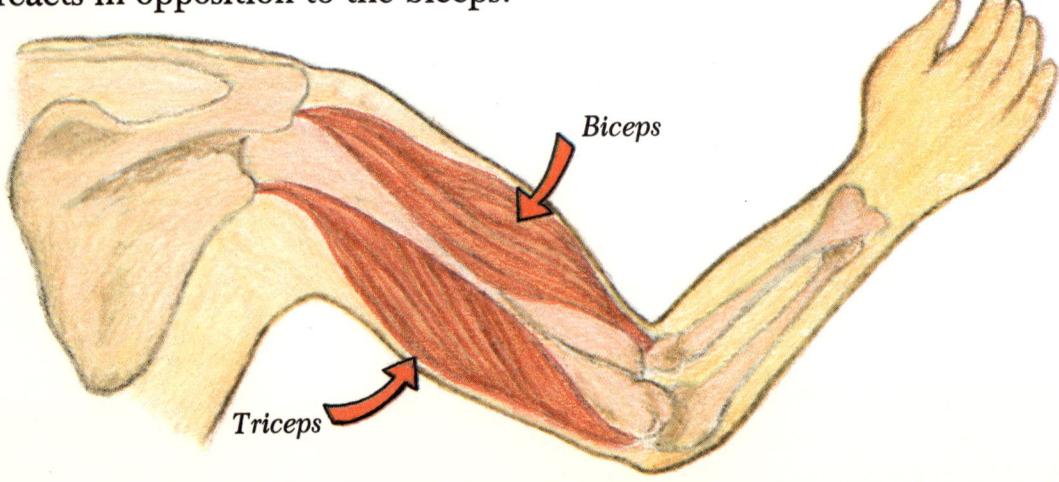

Muscles of human arm

tropism (TROH·piz·um) *n.* the reaction of a plant's growth to a stimulus. For example, the tendency of plant roots to grow down in response to gravity is called *geotropism*. The tendency of a plant's leaves to face the sun as it grows is called *phototropism*.

Light source

Light source

troposphere (TROH·poh·sfeer) *n.* the lowest layer of the earth's atmosphere. Most weather takes place in the troposphere.

Stratosphere

Troposphere

trough (TRAHF) *n.* the low point between two waves.

n. a band of low air pressure between two high-pressure areas.

n. a dip or fold in layers of rock.

Fold in rocks

Trough

tsunami (tsoo·NAH·mee) *n.* a large, destructive tidal wave caused by a disturbance such as an earthquake on the ocean floor.

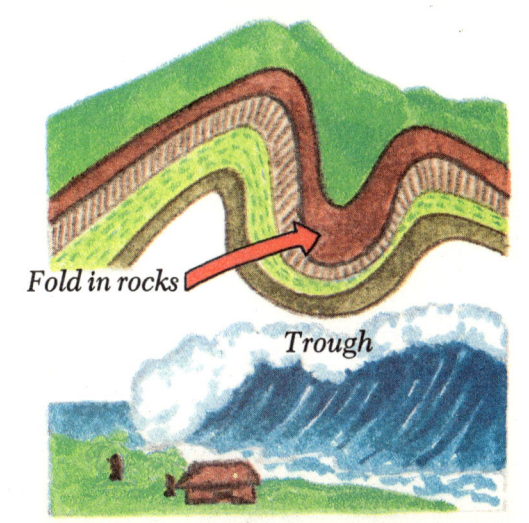

105

tuber (TOO·ber) *n.* the part of an underground plant stem that is swollen with stored food. A potato is a tuber.

tundra (TUN·druh) *n.* open plains in the arctic region that are treeless and have permanently frozen subsoil. Many animals, such as deer and wolves, live on tundras.

Musk ox

Arctic owl

Wolf

Caribou

Ermine

Arctic fox

Rock ptarmigan

Animals of the tundra

Uu

ultrasonic (ul·truh·SAHN·ik) *adj.* used to describe sound waves of a higher frequency than the human ear can hear.

ultraviolet (ul•truh•VY•uh•let) *adj.* light waves that are of a short wavelength and a high frequency, and which are invisible to the human eye. Ultraviolet rays from the sun cause sunburn.

unicellular (yew•nih•SELL•yew•ler) *adj.* describes a living thing made up of only one cell. An amoeba is unicellular.

unit (YEW•nit) *n.* a standard of measurement such as a foot, meter, or degree.

universe (YEW•nih•verss) *n.* everything that exists, known or unknown.

unstable (un•STAY•bul) *adj.* tending to break down or change easily.

Vv

vacuum (VAK•yewm) *n.* a completely empty space in which there are no molecules, atoms, or particles.

Van Allen belts (van AL•un BELTZ) *n.* two doughnut-shaped areas of charged particles within the earth's magnetosphere which trap deadly radiation from the sun.

vapor (VAY•per) *n.* a material in a gaseous state that at lower temperatures or higher pressures exists as a liquid or a solid. Water vapor in the air forms droplets as the air temperature drops.

variable star (VAYR•ee•uh•bul STAR) *n.* a star that changes in brightness over short periods of time.

vein (VAYN) *n.* a flexible tube that carries blood from body tissues to the heart.

Vein in rock

n. in rock, a streak or band of ore of a different type.

Vein in leaf

n. very fine tubes in the leaves of plants.

velocity (vuh·LAHS·ih·tee) *n.* the speed at which any substance or object is moving.

venom (VEN·um) *n.* a poisonous substance produced by certain animals such as snakes and spiders. Venom is usually injected through a bite or sting and is used to subdue or kill prey.

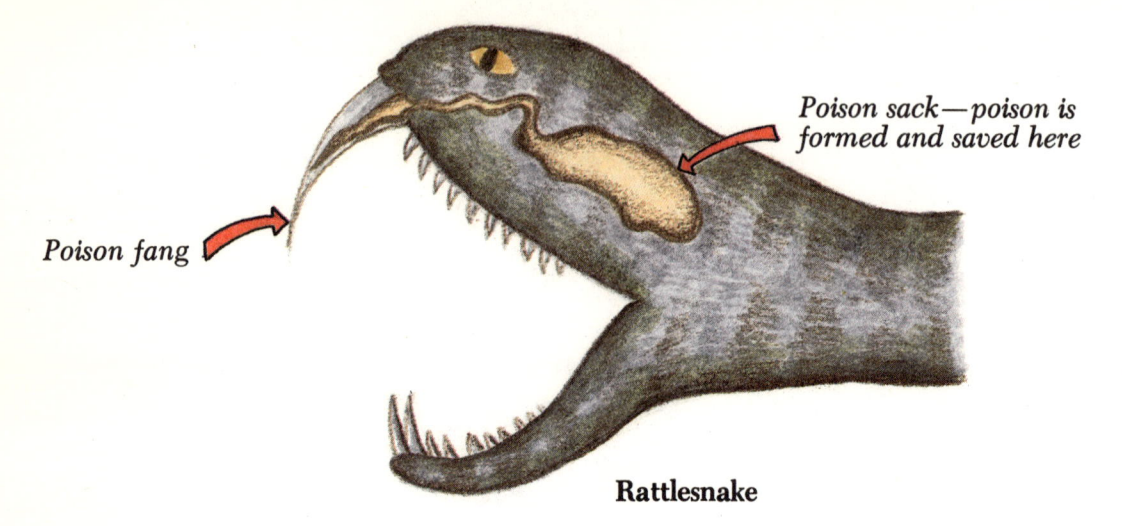

Poison sack—poison is formed and saved here

Poison fang

Rattlesnake

ventricle (VEN·trih·kul) *n.* one of two lower chambers on each side of the heart. From here blood is pumped into the arteries.

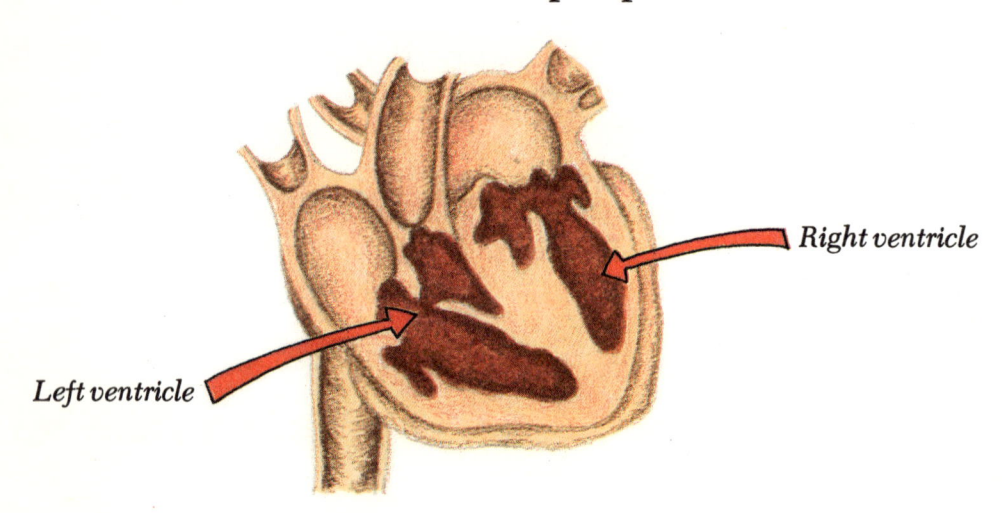

Right ventricle

Left ventricle

Cross section of a human heart

vertebra (VER·tuh·bruh) *n.* any of the small bones that make up the backbone, or spinal column.

vertebrate (VER·tuh·brayt) *n.* an animal with a backbone.

vertical (VERT•ih•kul) *adj.* at right angles to the horizon.

vibrate (VY•brayt) *v.* to move back and forth very quickly.

villi (VIL•eye) *n.* tiny, folded structures that line certain membranes. In the small intestine, villi absorb food and pass it into the bloodstream. Villi is plural. Villus is singular.

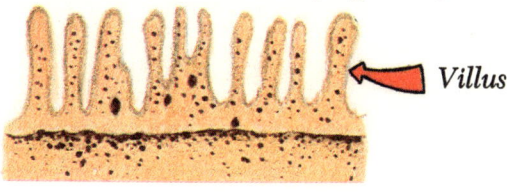

Villus

virus (VY•rus) *n.* ultramicroscopic pieces of living matter that can enter or infect other living things and change the way they work. Colds and flu are caused by viruses.

visible light (VIZ•uh•bul LYT) *n.* the part of the electromagnetic spectrum that has wavelengths visible as light to the human eye. The longest wavelengths of visible light appear as red, and the shortest appear as blue.

vitamin (VYT•uh•min) *n.* nutrient that helps the body stay healthy and work properly.

viviparous (vih•VIP•uh•rus) *adj.* giving birth to live offspring.

White-tailed doe with fawns

vocal cords (VOH·kul KORDZ) *n.* two stretchy bands of tissue in the throat. Vocal cords can vibrate and produce sounds when air passes between them.

volcano (vol·KAY·noh) *n.* a mountain or hill of lava and ash that has built up through eruptions from an opening in the surface of the earth. The Hawaiian Islands were formed from volcanoes.

n. an opening in the earth's surface through which lava and ash escape.

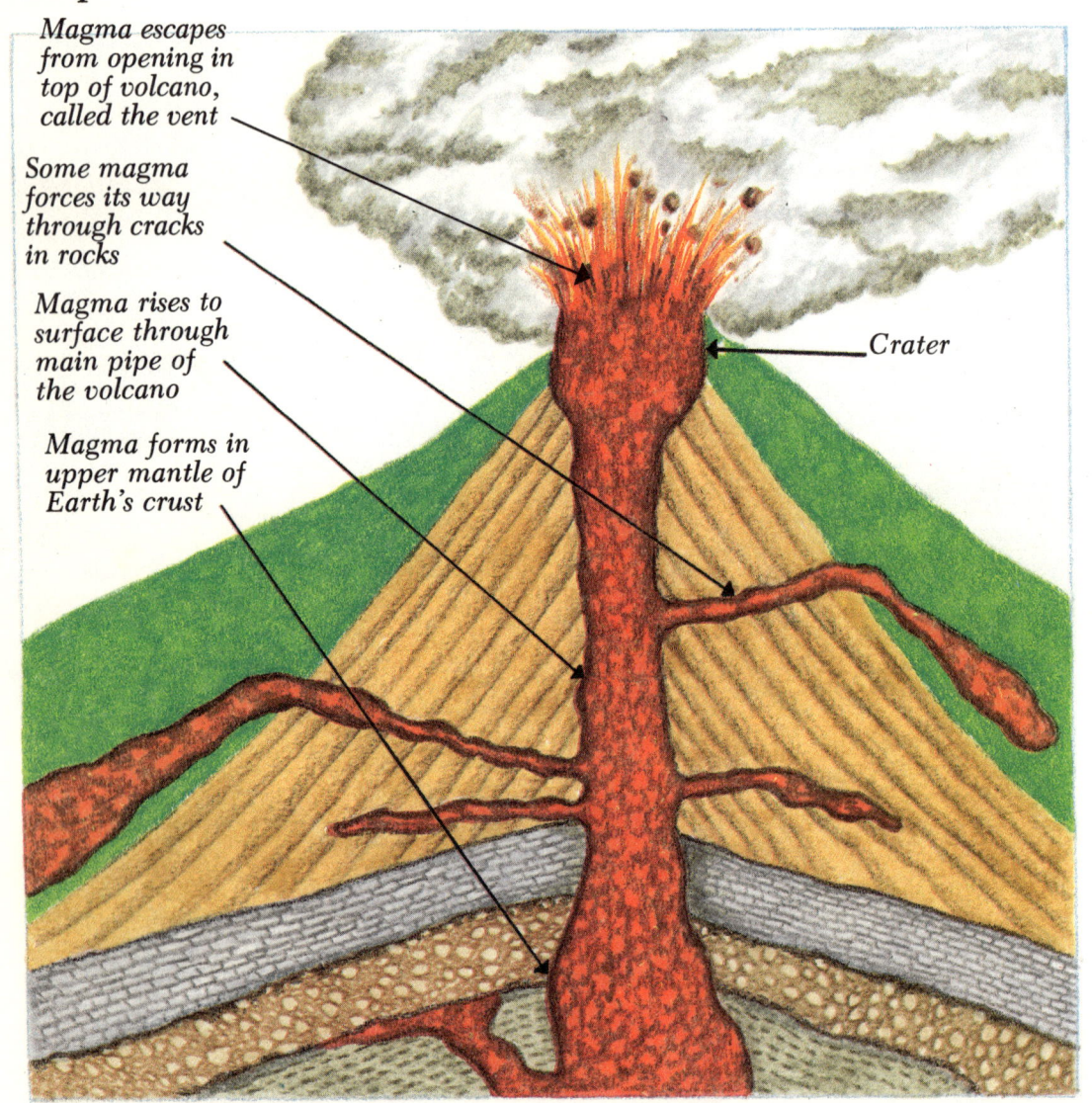

Magma escapes from opening in top of volcano, called the vent

Some magma forces its way through cracks in rocks

Magma rises to surface through main pipe of the volcano

Magma forms in upper mantle of Earth's crust

Crater

Cross section of a volcano

volt (VOLT) *n.* a unit of measurement of the force or pressure of an electrical current.

volume (VOL•yewm) *n.* the amount of space taken up by a substance or an object.

vortex (VOR•teks) *n.* a spinning mass of water or air that creates a vacuum at its center. Water running down a drain often forms a small vortex.

Diagram of a vortex   Vortex created when water runs down drain

Ww

warm-blooded (WARM-BLUD•ed) *adj.* describes an animal whose body temperature remains constant. Mammals and birds are warm-blooded; fish, amphibians, and reptiles are cold-blooded.

Bison's body temperature—the same in winter and summer

warm front (WARM FRUNT) *n.* the leading border of an advancing warm air mass.

111

water cycle (WAT•er SY•kul) *n.* the continuous movement of water between the earth and the atmosphere by evaporation, condensation, and precipitation.

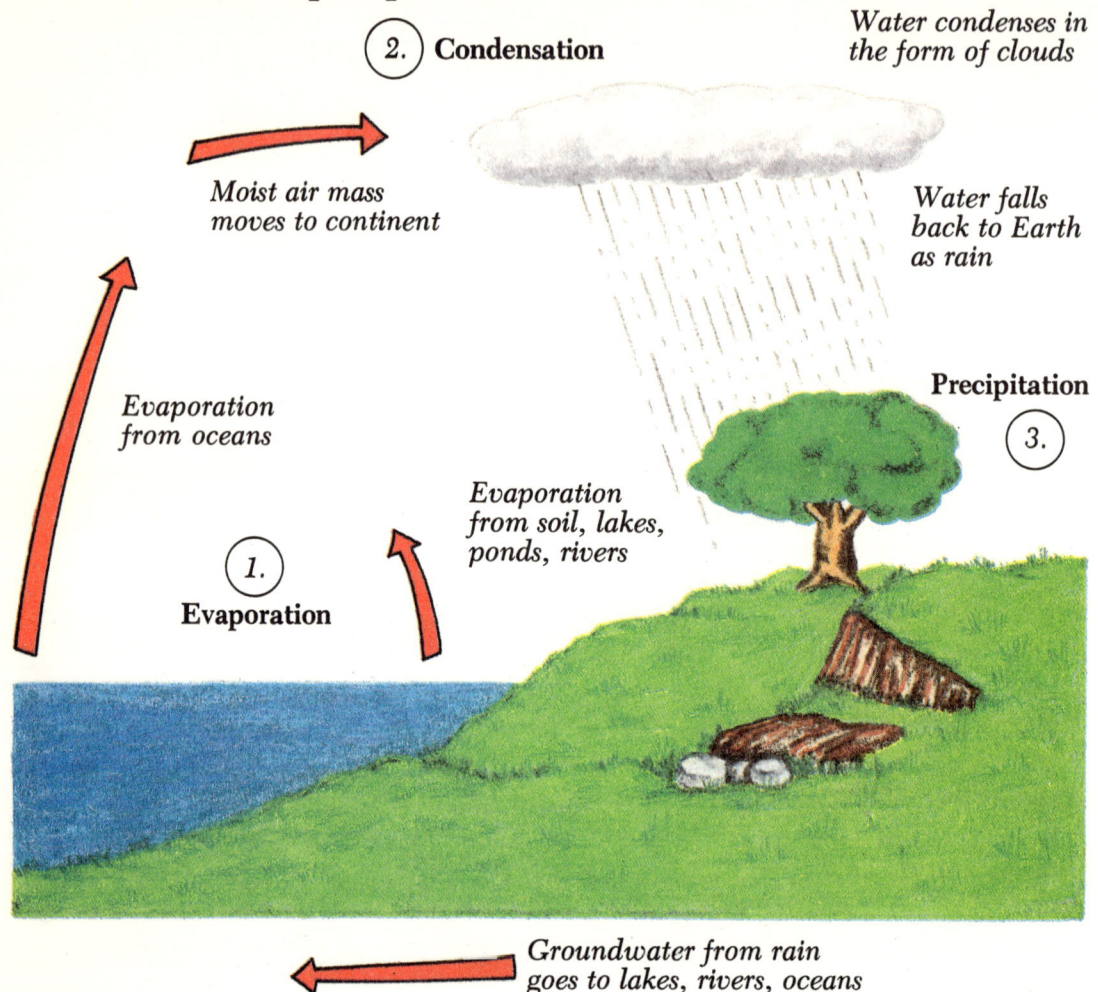

2. **Condensation**

Water condenses in the form of clouds

Moist air mass moves to continent

Water falls back to Earth as rain

Evaporation from oceans

Precipitation

3.

Evaporation from soil, lakes, ponds, rivers

1. **Evaporation**

Groundwater from rain goes to lakes, rivers, oceans

watershed (WAT•er•shed) *n.* an area where runoff from rain and snow divides and separates, draining ultimately into two different river systems. Watersheds are often found in high-ridge areas, where drainage flows down either side of the ridge.

water table (WAT•er TAY•bul) *n.* the underground area where groundwater collects because the rocks cannot absorb any more and the water cannot drain away.

water vapor (WAT•er VAY•per) *n.* water that has become a gas due to evaporation. Steam is superheated water vapor.

watt (WATT) *n.* a unit of measurement of electrical power.

wave (WAYV) *n.* a series of vibrations by which many types of energy travel.

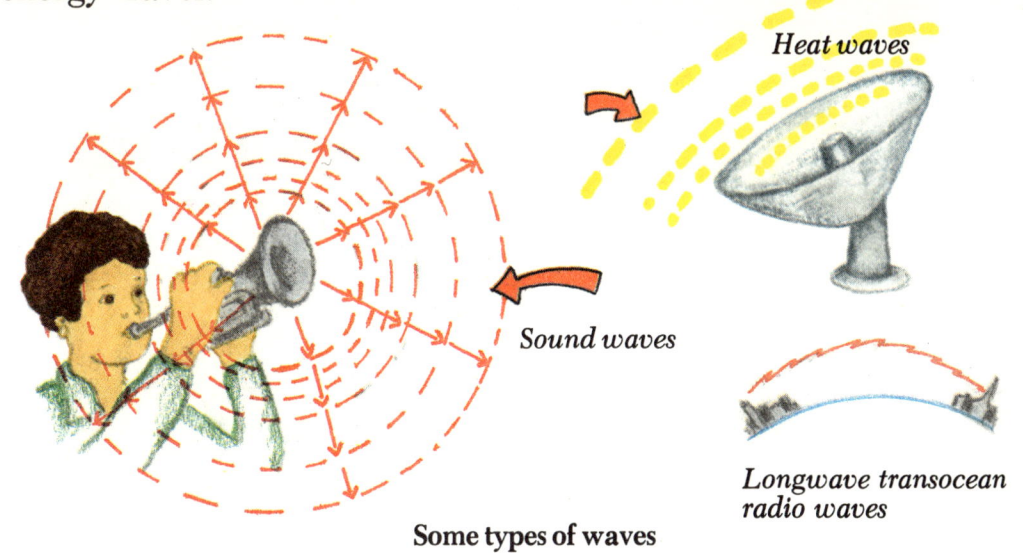

Heat waves

Sound waves

Longwave transocean radio waves

Some types of waves

n. a moving ridge of water on the surface of oceans or lakes, caused by the effects of wind or storms.

Beach   Breaker   Waves

Ocean waves breaking on the shore

wavelength (WAYV·layngth) *n.* the distance from the crest of one wave to the crest of the following wave.

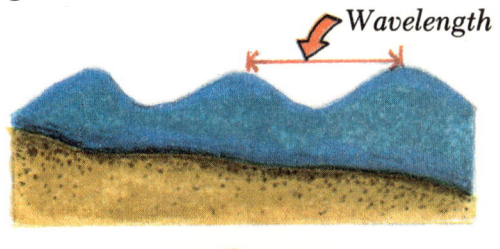

Wavelength

wax (WAKS) *n.* a waterproof, fatty substance. Bees produce a kind of wax structure in which they store honey. Glands in the human ear produce a form of wax to protect and clean the ear.

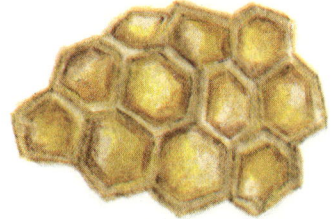

Section of a honeycomb

weather (WETH·er) *n.* conditions in the atmosphere including temperature, cloudiness, humidity, and barometric pressure.

113

weathering (WETH•er•ing) *n.* the wearing away of rock by wind, water, temperature changes, and other erosive forces.

wedge (WEJ) *n.* an inclined plane that is thick at one end and has a sharp edge at the other end. Wedges are often used to split things apart, raise heavy weights, or hold things firmly in place.

Wedges

weight (WAYT) *n.* the measure of how much gravitational force is exerted on an object or substance.

wheel and axle (WEEL and AK•sul) *n.* a simple machine made up of a wheel with a rod through the center. The wheel rotates on the rod, which is called the axle. Sometimes the wheel is grooved and has a rope attached to it. Many machines have wheels and axles.

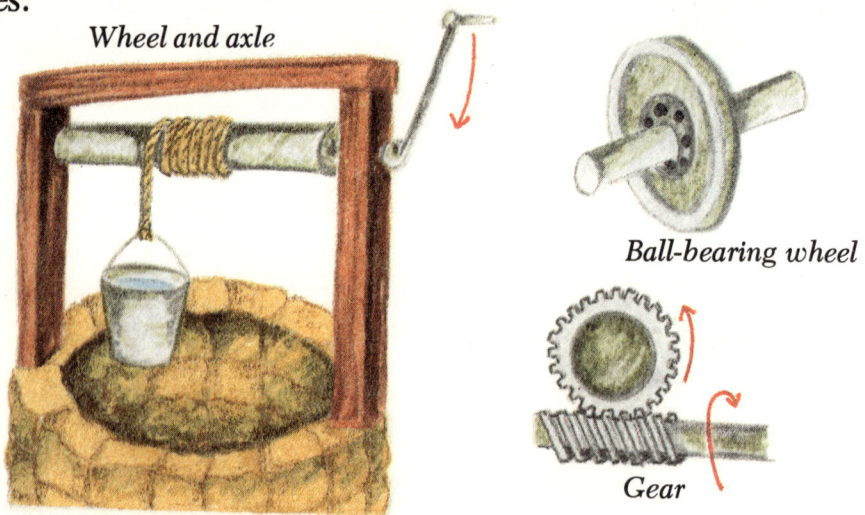

Wheel and axle

Ball-bearing wheel

Gear

Simple wheel and axle machines

white dwarf (WHYT DWARF) *n.* a small, dense, dim star that has passed through its red-giant stage and has no nuclear fuel left.

wind (WIND) *n.* streams of air that flow from one place to another due to many factors. A very important factor is uneven heating of the earth's atmosphere.

work (WERK) *n.* the energy expended when a force acts. The amount of work done equals the force applied to an object times the distance the object was moved by the force.

Xx

X-ray (EKS-ray) *n.* a form of electromagnetic energy with a very short wavelength and high frequency. X-rays are able to pass through certain materials, such as skin and muscle, more easily than others, such as bone. Because of this ability, special pictures can be taken of the human body to show the bones inside.

xylem (ZY•lum) *n.* a tissue that helps support a plant and carries water and minerals from the roots to the leaves.

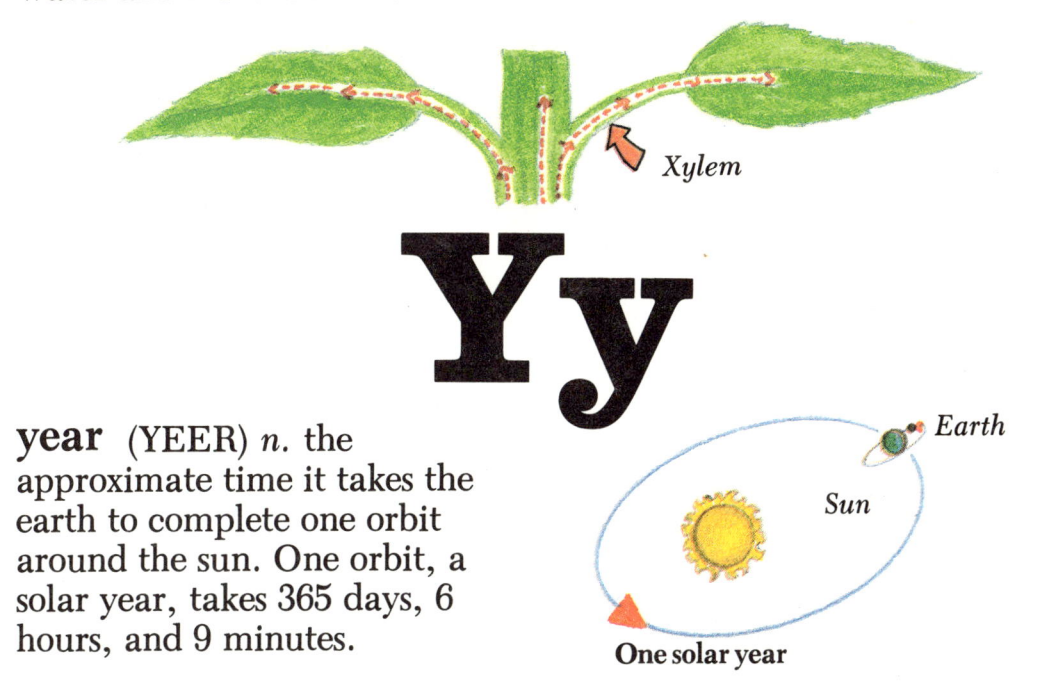

Xylem

Yy

year (YEER) *n.* the approximate time it takes the earth to complete one orbit around the sun. One orbit, a solar year, takes 365 days, 6 hours, and 9 minutes.

Earth
Sun
One solar year

yeast (YEEST) *n.* a fungus that feeds on and breaks down sugar in certain substances, producing carbon dioxide. Yeast is used in baking to make dough rise. Some yeasts produce alcohol as a by-product and are used in brewing.

yolk (YOHK) *n.* the thick yellow substance inside of an egg that is rich in fat and protein and is used as food by the developing embryo.

Yolk

Zz

zenith (ZEE•nith) *n.* a point in the sky directly overhead of an observer.

zero (ZEE•roh) *n.* a symbol that holds the place of a number but does not represent a quantity. The number between the set of all negative numbers and the set of all positive numbers (... −3, −2, −1, 0, +1, +2, +3...).

zone (ZOHN) *n.* an area that has special characteristics common throughout the entire area. For example, there are earthquake zones, weather zones, and tidal zones.

zoology (zoh•OL•uh•jee) *n.* the scientific study of animal life.

Researcher observing gorilla